Paper Stars

25 FESTIVE DECORATIONS FOR EVERY OCCASION

Karen-Marie Fabricius

First published 2017 by
Guild of Master Craftsman Publications Ltd
Castle Place, 166 High Street, Lewes,
East Sussex BN7 1XU

ISBN 978 1 78494 337 0

Publisher Jonathan Bailey
Production Manager Jim Bulley
Senior Project Editor Dominique Page
Editor Judith Chamberlain-Webber
Managing Art Editor Gilda Pacitti
Designer Ginny Zeal
Photographers Claus Bradsted & Kent Stokholm Petersen

Set in Fira Sans
Colour origination by GMC Reprographics
Printed and bound in Malaysia

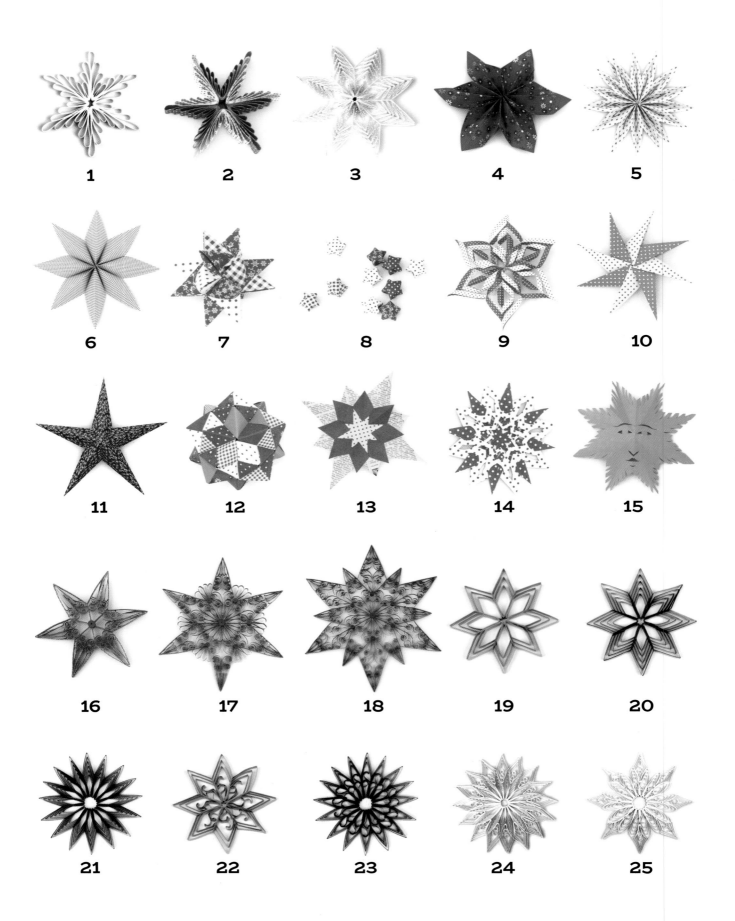

1

2

3

4

5

6

7

8

9

10

11

12

13

14

15

16

17

18

19

20

21

22

23

24

25

Contents

Introduction

For almost a year I have lived among the stars. It has been a delightful journey through the paper universe, from one star to the next. From the moment I had the idea to produce a book of 25 paper stars I have been folding, plaiting, cutting and quilling stars. I hope that you will have as much fun making them as I did. If you are new to star-making, you will find all the techniques explained at the back of the book. Difficulty ratings beside each project will guide you and help you to build up your skills and confidence. Soon enough, you'll be able to make even the most complex-looking stars. Really, they are all very simple – once you know how!

Karen-Marie Fabricius

Comb Quilling Stars

A COMB IS A POPULAR QUILLING TOOL AND IT'S EASY
FOR BEGINNERS TO USE. THE HERLEV AND THE SLIGHTLY
LARGER COPENHAGEN ARE SIMPLE STARS AND A GOOD
PLACE TO START. TRY USING DIFFERENT COLOURS AND
WIDTHS OF PAPER. THEN, WHEN YOU FEEL CONFIDENT
WITH THE TECHNIQUE, YOU CAN PROGRESS TO THE
MORE DIFFICULT ÅRHUS.

Herlev

★★★★★

Actual size

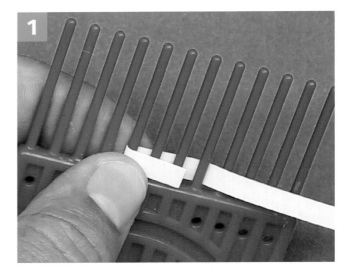

MATERIALS
Paper strips x 6, measuring 8⅞ x ³⁄₁₆in (225 x 5mm)
Glue

TOOLS
Comb
Measuring board
Pins

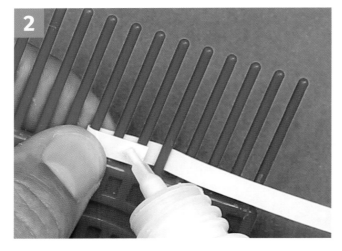

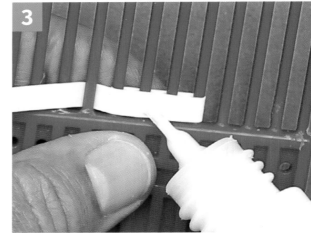

1 Hold the comb in one hand. Take the end of one strip and bring it round the fifth tooth from the left from back to front. Fold the paper so that it fits over three teeth. Bring the long end up four teeth from the right.

2 Put a small dab of glue at the end of the short fold.

3 Bring the long end of the paper strip over the fold and behind the comb. Bring the strip up around the next tooth to the side and add a small dab of glue at the central point.

4–5 Take the strip behind the next tooth on the right, then bring to the front and secure with glue as before. Repeat once more on each side.

6 Slide the paper off the comb and bend it in the middle so you have three matching loops facing each other. Take care not to squeeze the tops of the loops; just press at the base.

7 Make a loop with the strip end, gluing the tip of it to the base. This loop is a bit longer than the other three loops. Repeat Steps 1–7 five more times so you have six identical figures.

8 Glue the units together in pairs then pin and glue them together on the measuring board using the pink lines as a guide.

9 Leave a space at the base of each section so that the central star shape will be formed.

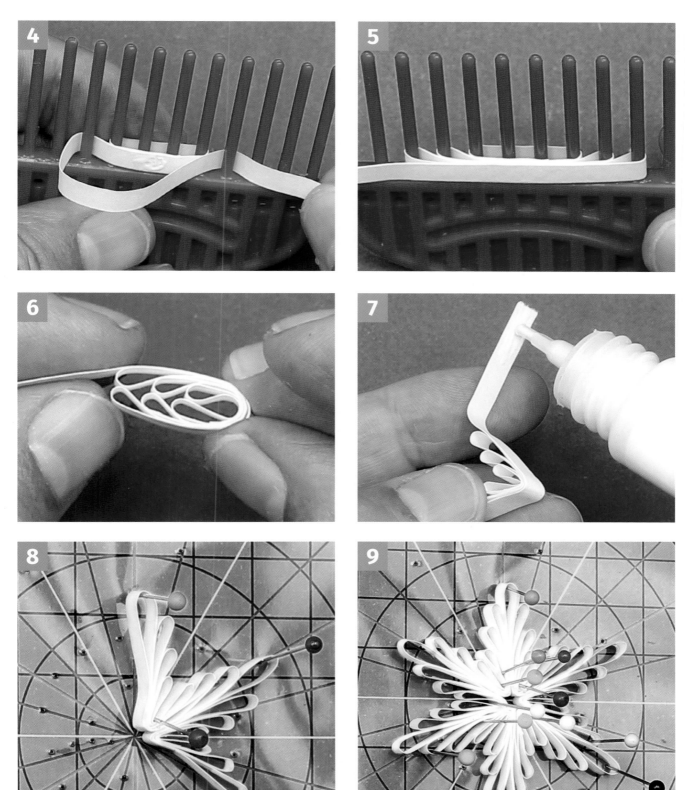

Copenhagen

★★★★★

Actual size

MATERIALS

6 x paper strips in two contrasting
  colours, measuring 8⅞ x 3/16in
  (225 x 5mm)
Glue

TOOLS

Comb
Measuring board
Pins

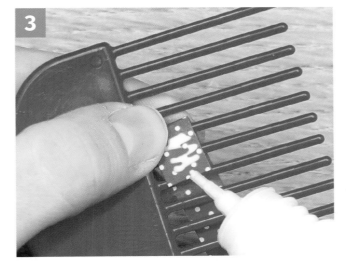

1–2 Hold the comb in one hand. Take the end of one strip and bring it round the fifth tooth from the left from back to front.

3 Fold the paper so that it fits over three teeth. Put a small dab of glue at the end of the short fold.

4 Bring the long end of the paper strip up four teeth in from the right, over the fold and behind the comb four teeth from the left.

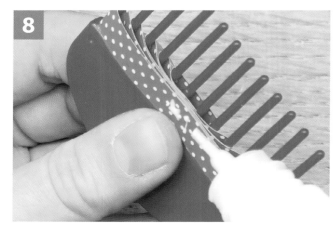

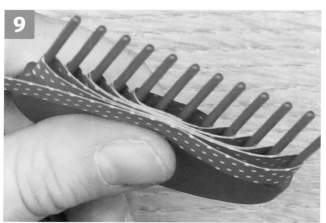

5–6 Wrap the strip around the next tooth on the left, then bring it to the front and secure with glue at the central point.

7 Take the strip behind the next tooth on the right, then bring to the front and secure with glue as before.

8–9 Continue to wind from side to side, increasing the size of the folds each time by using the next pair of teeth on the comb. Glue at the central point after each fold. Make sure you don't wind the paper tightly, otherwise you will find it difficult to remove it from the comb.

10 Slide the paper off the comb and bend it in the middle so you have five matching loops facing each other. Take care not to squeeze the tops of the loops; just press at the base.

11–12 Make a loop in the long strip end slightly longer than the other five loops and apply a dot of glue to the end of the strip to secure the loop to the base. Repeat Steps 1–12 with all your strips of paper.

13–14 Glue the units together in pairs, placing alternate colours next to each other.

15 Pin and glue the pairs together onto the measuring board using the pink lines as a guide. Leave a space at the base of each section to form the central star shape.

rhus

★★★★★

Actual size

MATERIALS
68 x paper strips, measuring
   17¾ x ³⁄₁₆in (450 x 5mm)
16 x paper strips, measuring
   17¾ x ⅛in (450 x 3mm) (optional)
Glue
⅛in (3mm) double-sided tape

TOOLS
Comb
Measuring board
Scissors
Pins

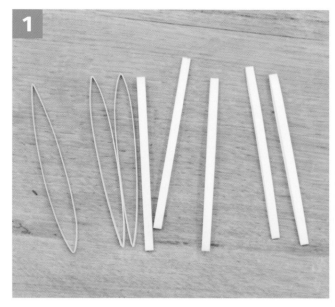

1 Make eight Loop A units with the ³⁄₁₆in (5mm) paper strips (see page 131) and flatten so both ends are pointed.

2–3 Stack the units on top of each other then fold in half one way and then in half the other way, so they form a diamond shape.

4 Glue the units together one by one along one side to make a star.

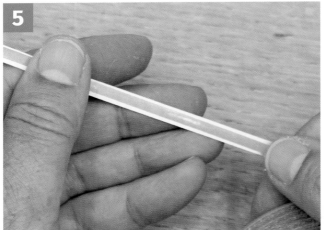

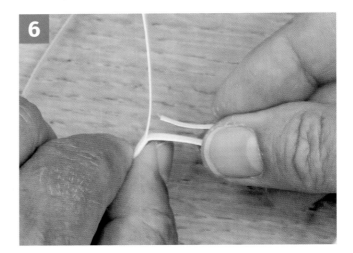

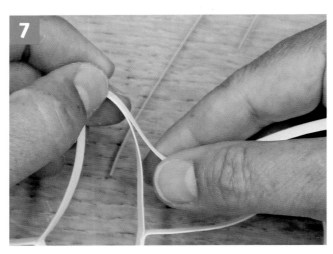

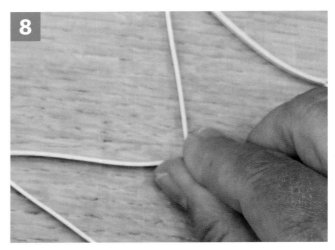

5–8 To reinforce the star, stick double-sided tape to two of the ³⁄₁₆in (5mm) strips and fasten them around the perimeter of the star. Make sure the paper is stuck all the way to the bottom of each 'valley'. This may skew the star – if so, gently straighten it again.

9 Pin the star onto your measuring board using the green ⅛th line.

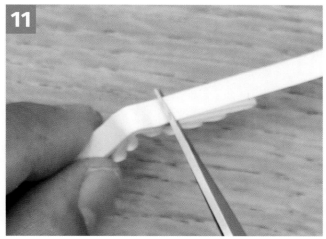

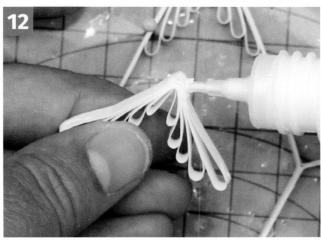

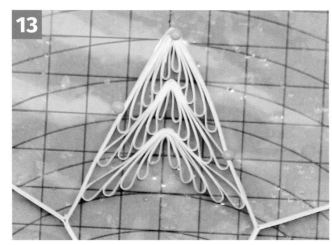

10–11 To fill each unit, make seven wing shapes using ³⁄₁₆in (5mm) strips (see page 137 for instructions).

12–14 Use the circles marked on the measuring board to position the wings accurately. Glue the wings into position as shown and use pins to make sure they stay in place until the glue is dry.

★ TIP ★

For an elegant finish you can make two extra Copenhagen stars with eight points. For these stars you use the ⅛in (3mm) strips. To create a 3D effect, place a star at each side of the centre. The Århus star is also nice without the extra decoration – if you don't want to make it then the ⅛in (3mm) strips are not needed!

Folded Stars

I LOVE TO FOLD CLASSIC STARS, BUT I ESPECIALLY LOVE
TO CREATE, REMAKE, TWIST AND TURN THE PAPER TO SEE
WHAT WILL HAPPEN. JUST OCCASIONALLY, A NEW STAR IS
BORN AND SUCH A STAR IS ESBJERG. ESBJERG IS A FUN
DESIGN AND LOOKS ITS BEST WHEN IT'S MADE IN SMALL
PAPER SIZES. RIBE IS A CLASSIC DESIGN AND BEAUTIFUL
FOR WINDOW DECORATIONS. VARDE IS A QUICK MAKE
AND LOOKS GREAT WHEN HUNG IN LARGE GROUPS OR
AS AN EYE-CATCHING TABLE DECORATION.

Esbjerg

★★★★★

Actual size

4

ESBJERG

MATERIALS
3 x paper squares, measuring
  4 x 4in (100 x 100mm)
Matching cotton thread
Glue

TOOLS
Scissors
Bone folder (optional)

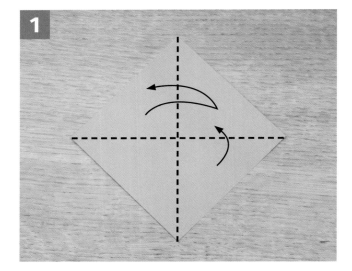

1–2 With the paper square placed diagonally in front of you and right side down, fold in half horizontally and vertically to make triangle shapes. A bone folder can be used. Open the square out again.

3–4 Fold the bottom corner of the square upwards to the middle horizontal fold. Repeat with the top corner and then open out again.

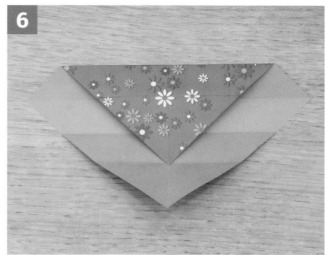

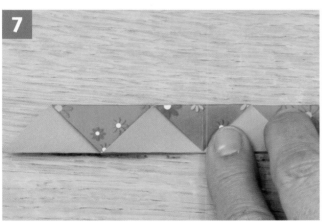

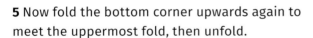

5 Now fold the bottom corner upwards again to meet the uppermost fold, then unfold.

6 Fold the top corner downwards to the lowermost fold then unfold. You should now have five folds. Repeat Steps 1–6 with the other two squares.

7 Open out the paper. Starting at one edge, pleat the folds (folding one way then the other) to form a narrow strip. The two folds either side of the central fold should end up folding the other way. Fold the two pointed ends down to meet the longer edge. Repeat with the other two paper squares.

8–9 Fold the strip in half and cut a ⅛in (2mm) slit into each side of the fold line for the thread.

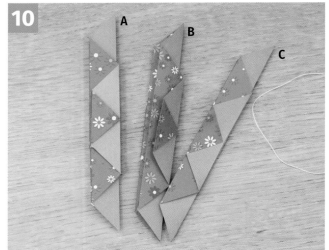

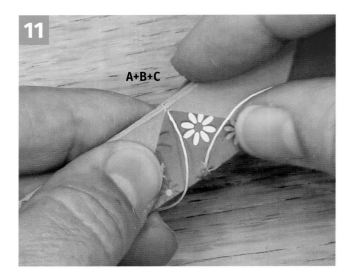

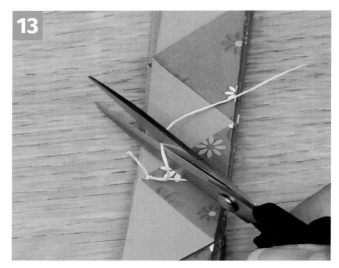

10–13 Fold the other two strips the same way and put all three together. Tie them together at the centre slits with thread. Cut off any loose ends.

14–15 Fold the three pieces in half together. Apply a small amount of glue to the two triangles either side of the fold line then fold over as shown and stick together.

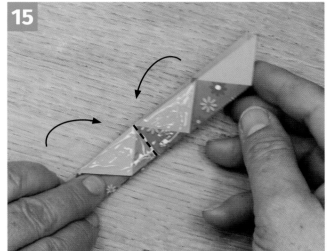

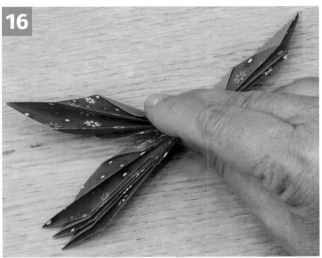

16 Repeat Step 15 to join the next two strips together.

17–18 Only glue the last two strips together when the first has fully dried. Stretch out the points carefully.

Ribe

★★★★★

Actual size

MATERIALS

2 x paper squares, measuring
  4 x 4in (100 x 100mm)
Matching cotton thread
Double-sided tape
Glue (optional)

TOOLS

Scissors

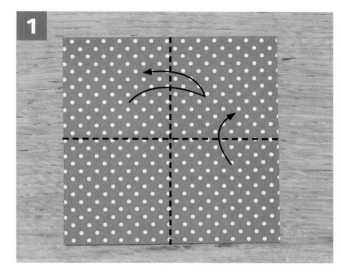

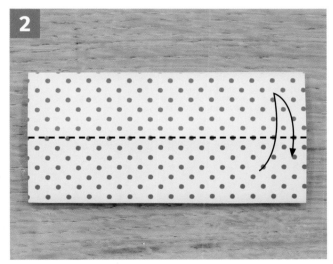

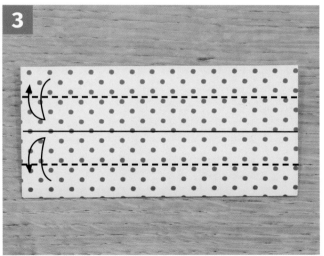

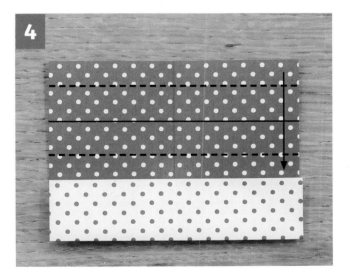

1 With the paper square placed right side down, fold in half vertically to make a rectangle and then fold in half horizontally.

2 Fold in half horizontally again to make a thinner rectangle, then open out to a half square again.

3–4 Now fold both top and bottom edges in so they meet at the centre fold. Open the square out and you should now have seven folds.

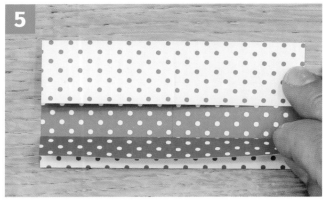

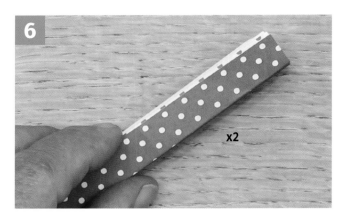

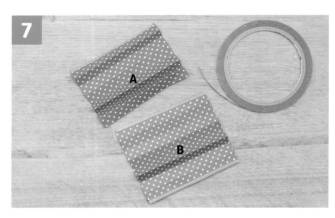

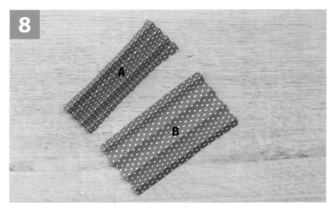

5–6 Starting at one edge, pleat the folds (folding one way then the other) to form a narrow strip. Repeat steps 1–5 with the other square.

7 With the paper right side down, stick a strip of double-sided tape down both edges of one square parallel to the fold. Repeat on one edge of the other square.

8 Remove the top layer of the tape on one edge of the first square then place the untaped edge of the second square on top of it with wrong sides together. Make sure the line where the squares are joined is folded to form a valley.

9–10 Fold one of the corners at an angle as shown. Cut it off and use the cut piece as a template for cutting the other side.

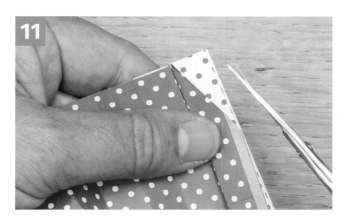

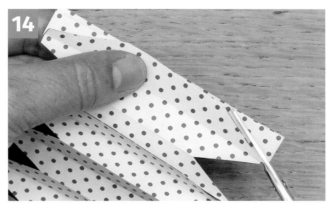

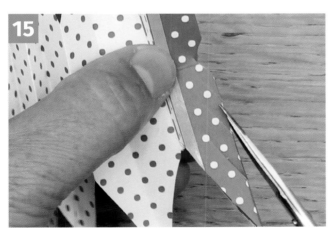

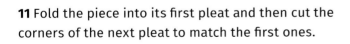

11 Fold the piece into its first pleat and then cut the corners of the next pleat to match the first ones.

12–14 Repeat this for one square then fold over and repeat for the other square. Continue folding and cutting until you reach the end of the squares.

15 Now cut a little triangular notch in the middle on both sides for the thread.

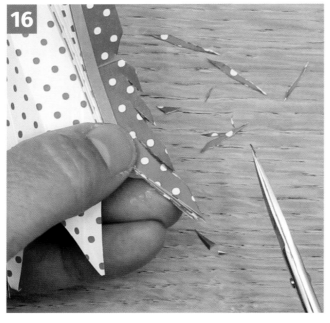

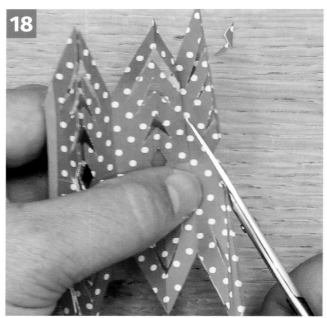

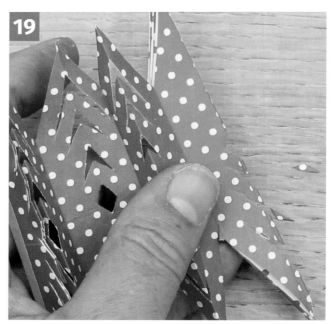

16–18 Cut larger slits in the folded edges, either side of the notch, cutting two or three pleats at a time and using the first slits you cut as a guide. Try to make them equally spaced above and below.

19 You can open out the star to check how it looks.

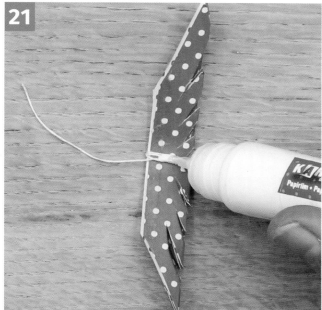

20–21 Tie the star together with thread around the middle. Cut off the loose ends. The knot can be glued to make sure it stays.

22–23 Remove the double-sided tape and stick the edges of the star together, then spread out the points of the star.

Varde

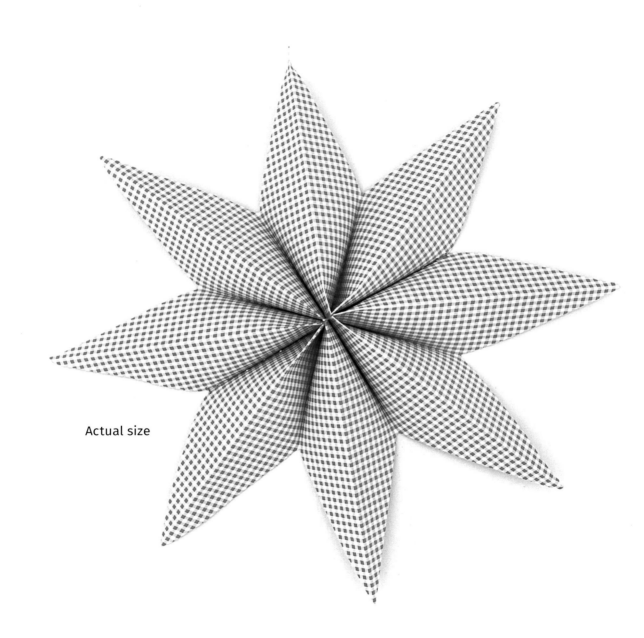

Actual size

MATERIALS

1 x paper square, measuring 6 x 6in
   (150 x 150mm)
Matching cotton thread
Glue

TOOLS

Scissors
Bone folder

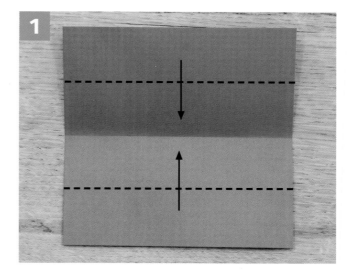

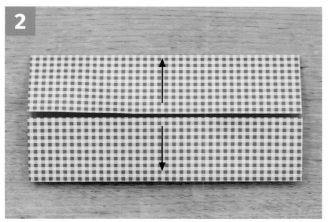

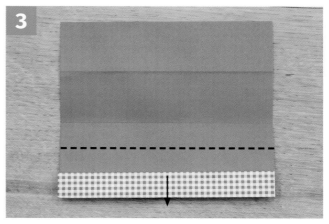

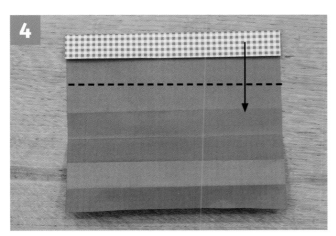

1–2 With the paper square placed right side down, fold in half horizontally to make a rectangle then open out and fold both edges in to meet at the centre fold.

3–4 Now fold each horizontal section in half again, giving you eight folds.

★ TIP ★

This star is folded in 6 x 6in (150 x 150mm) paper. However, you can make it in different sizes but you will need to adjust the measurement in step 7.

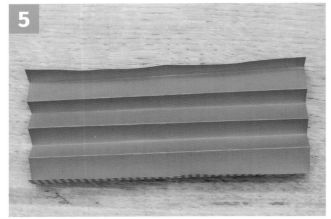

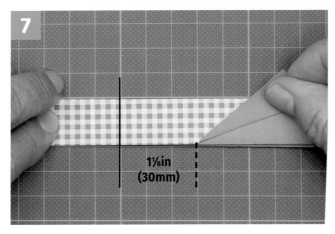

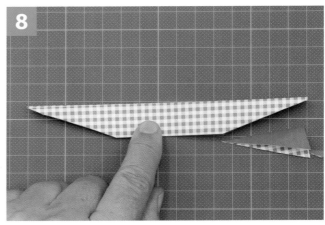

1⅛in
(30mm)

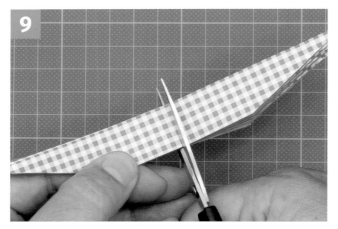

5 Starting at one edge, pleat the folds (folding one way then the other) to form a narrow strip.

6 Fold the square in half at right angles to the pleats to form a centre fold.

7 Measure 1⅛in (30mm) from the centre fold and make a small mark. Fold the corner from this mark up to the top edge as shown to make a point. Repeat on the other side.

8 Cut along the fold lines through all of the paper layers.

9–10 Make approx. ⅛in (3mm) slit on each side of the fold line for the thread. Tie the thread around and cut off any loose ends.

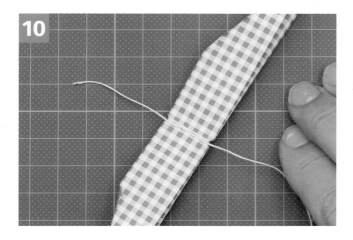

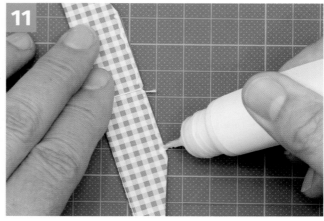

11 Apply a fine line of glue to the shorter edge of the shape.

12 Fold the two edges together. Press together.

13–14 When the first half has dried, carefully stretch the star shape out and glue the other half together.

15 Spread out the star points, using the bone folder.

Woven Stars

THIS GROUP OF CLASSIC STARS IS ETERNALLY POPULAR.
IN DENMARK, THE FIRST STAR IN THIS GROUP, THE FROEBEL
STAR, IS ASSOCIATED WITH A PROPER DANISH CHRISTMAS,
AND IS OFTEN USED AS A DECORATION ON THE TREE.
THE LUCKY STAR COMES FROM CHINA AND IS USED ALL
YEAR ROUND TO BRING GOOD LUCK. IT IS QUICK AND FUN
TO MAKE ONCE YOU GET THE HANG OF IT. SWING STAR IS
A CHEERFUL, WHIMSICAL STAR, WHICH CAN BE MADE OUT
OF LOTS OF DIFFERENT PAPERS.

Froebel

★★★★★

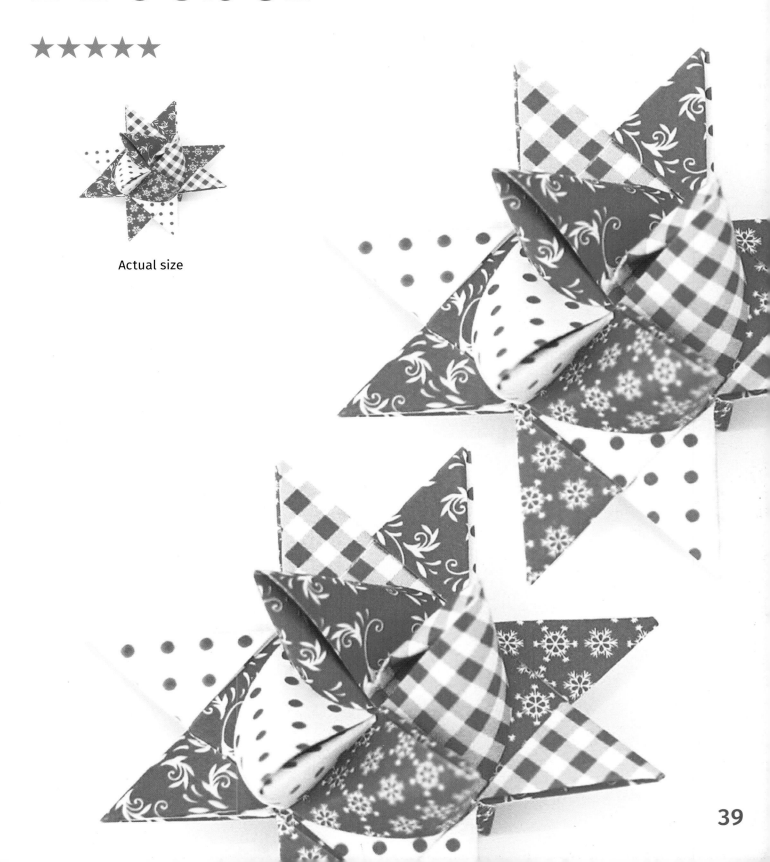

Actual size

MATERIALS
4 x paper strips, in different colours/
patterns, measuring 17¾ x ⅜in
(450 x 10mm)

TOOLS
Scissors

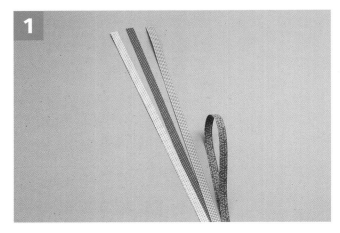

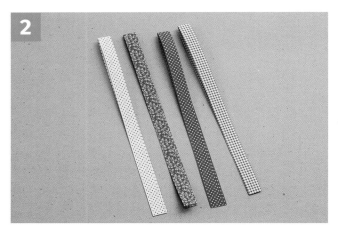

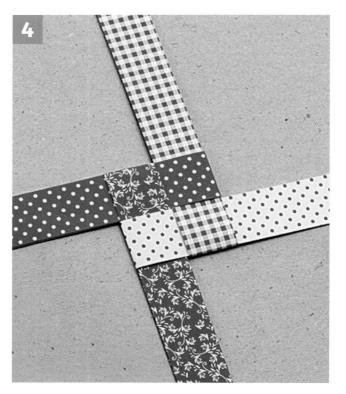

1–2 Fold the strips in half as shown.

3–4 Place the fold of one strip over the bottom 'leg' of one of the other strips. Continue plaiting the strips together, as shown in picture 4, over the 'leg' of one strip and then under the 'leg' of the next. Pull the ends together carefully to form a plaited square.

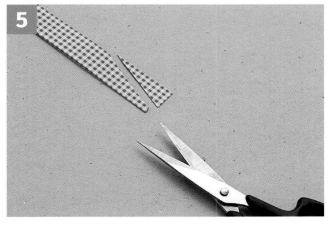

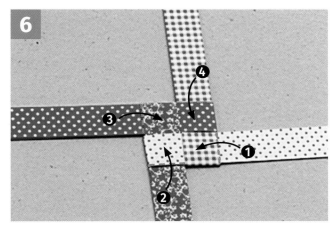

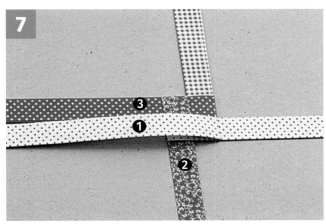

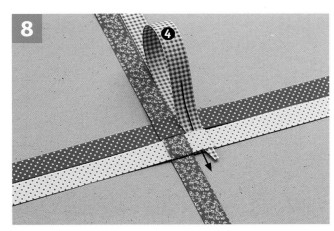

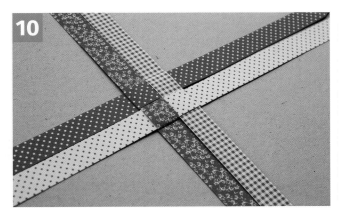

5 Cut the ends of one of the strips to make a point. This will make it easier to pull through. Do the same with the other strips – you can use the cut piece as a template.

6–9 Fold the upper 'leg' of each strip backwards over the central square shape in turn, as shown, and weave the last 'leg' (4) under the first strip (1)

to lock the strips in place. You should now have two parallel strips (one longer than the other) coming out from each square.

10–11 Fold one of the shorter strips backwards at an angle, as shown overleaf, so that the strip lies parallel with the others.

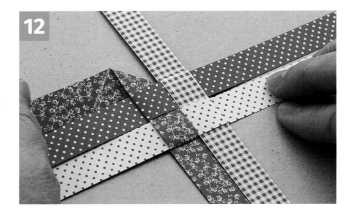

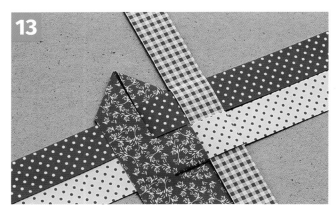

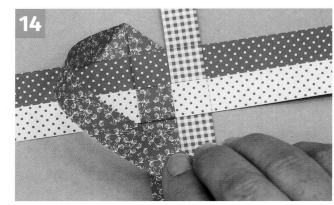

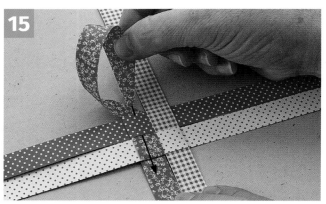

12–13 Fold again, as shown, to make a 90-degree turn and bring the 'leg' over the top to lie parallel with the next set of strips. Make sure there is an approx. 1/16in (1mm) gap.

14–17 Take the end of the strip and turn it backwards through 180 degrees so that you can insert it under the top left-hand 'pocket'.

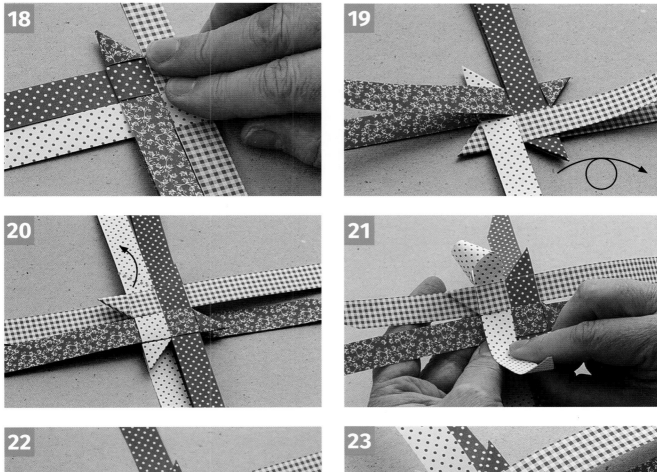

18 Flatten the triangle formed.

19–21 Turn over and fold the remaining three points in the same way. You should now have two strips coming out from each square on top of each other.

22–23 Fold the top four strips backwards over the central shape as shown.

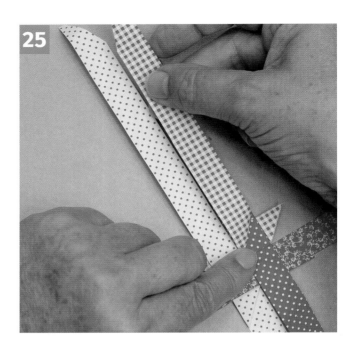

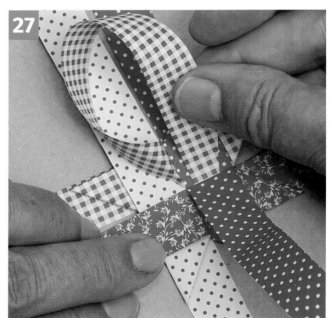

24–27 To make the upper points, take the top right-hand strip and fold it up and away from you, but do not crease the fold. Now take the end of the strip and turn it through 180 degrees and insert the end into the 'pocket' below the next strip along clockwise, ensuring that the top of the strip remains uppermost. Pull gently through to form the point shown in picture 28.

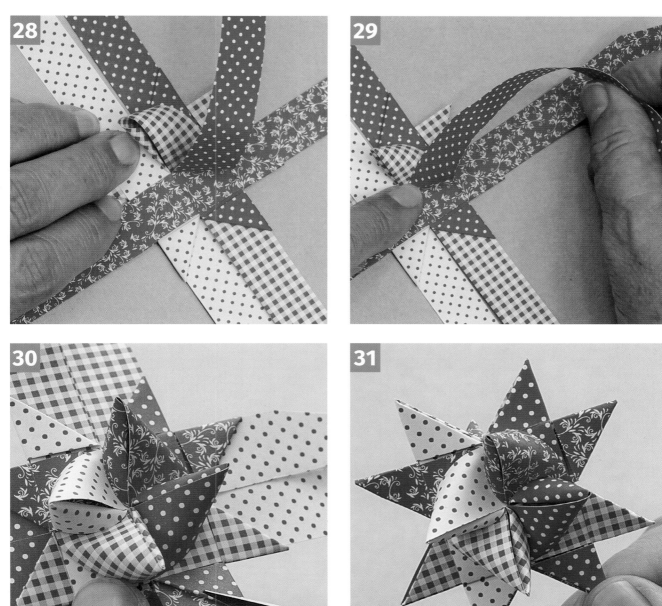

28–31 Continue to do the same for the other three strips. Turn over and repeat with the remaining strips. Pull each tip gently through and snip off the unwanted ends.

Lucky

★★★★★

Actual size

MATERIALS
1 x paper strip, measuring
17¾ x ⅜in (450 x 10mm)

TOOLS
Scissors
Bone folder

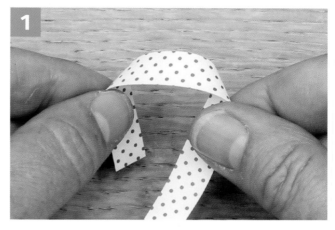

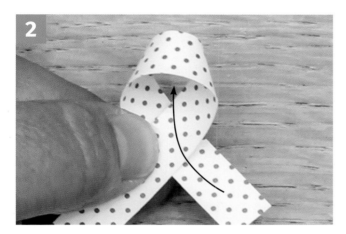

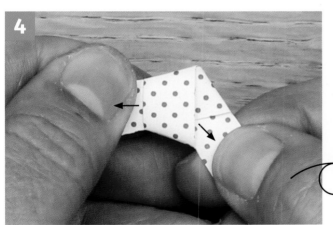

★ TIP ★
Different widths can be used for the Lucky star.

1–5 Make a knot, leaving an end approx. ⅜in (10mm) long. Pull carefully and press flat. Turn, fold the short end and put it in the 'pocket'.

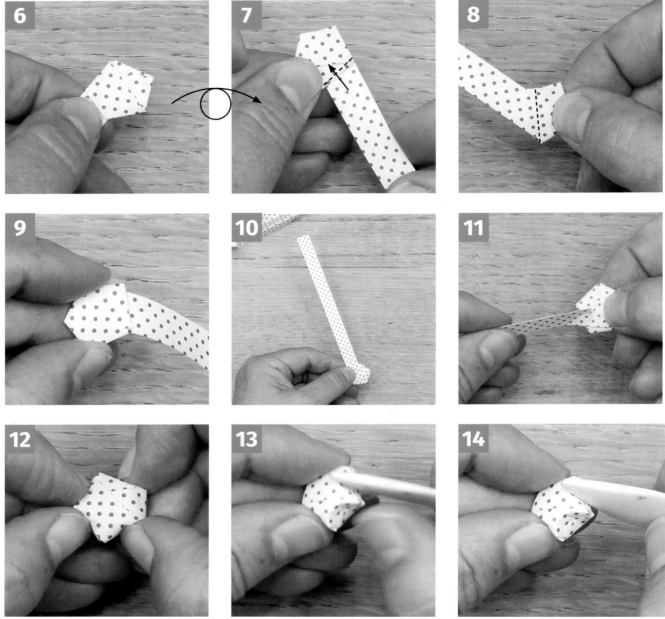

6 Turn again and fold the long end so that a pentagon is formed.

7–11 Continue to wind around. Make sure you follow the edges so that the pentagon is visible all the time. When you feel that it is as thick as a coin, stop – there will be about 5–6in (120–160mm) left. Cut or tear off the end and tuck it into the 'pocket'.

12–14 To make the shape three-dimensional, press hard between the points with your fingertips and nails, preferably more than one side at a time. It helps to use a bone folder.

Swing

★★★★★

Actual size

MATERIALS
6 x paper squares, measuring
   4 x 4in (100 x 100mm)
Glue

TOOLS
Craft knife
Ruler
Cutting mat
Bone folder

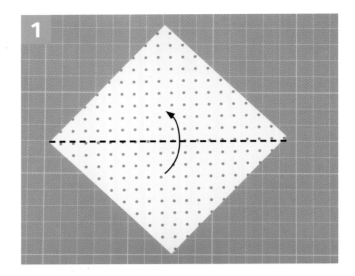

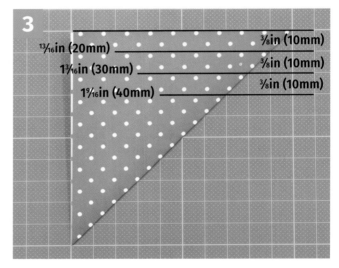

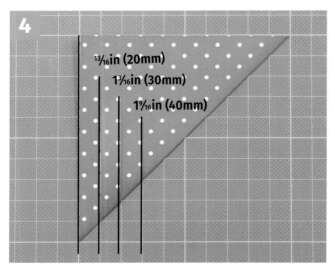

1 Place one of the paper squares right side down and diagonally in front of you onto a cutting board that has ⅜in (10mm) squares (these will be used for measuring). Fold in half to make a triangle then place with the right angle to your left.

2–4 Using the craft knife and ruler, make a series of three cuts ⅜in (10mm) apart, parallel to the top edge and at the lengths shown. Turn the triangle over so the right angle is at the top left-hand corner again and repeat the cuts. Repeat with the remaining five squares.

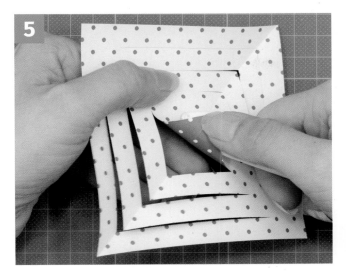

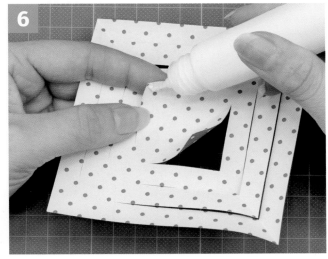

5–7 Open out the square. Using a bone folder, curl the innermost triangles in towards each other as shown and glue together at the tip, using the bone folder to press against.

8–9 Turn the square over and curl the next strips towards each other, and glue together. Add a dab of glue to the outside corners of the square.

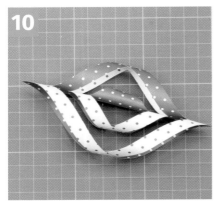

10 Curl the remaining strip in the opposite direction to the last one to complete the shape, then repeat with the other five squares.

11–13 Glue two of the shapes together at their widest points, then join a third in the same way.

14 Glue the pointed ends together. Repeat with the other three shapes.

15–16 Glue the two halves together at the central point then join at the widest points of the shapes.

Origami Stars

I FIND THAT ORIGAMI EXERCISES THE BRAIN AND THE FINGERS. IT'S GREAT TO LEARN AND CREATE NEW STARS, BUT IT'S ALSO VERY SATISFYING WHEN YOU'VE FINALLY TRAINED YOUR FINGERS TO FOLD THE STARS WITHOUT YOU HAVING TO THINK! THE STAR OF FAABORG AND THE STAR OF SVENDBORG ARE CLASSIC MODULAR ORIGAMI. THEY CAN EASILY BE MADE IN DIFFERENT COLOURS AND SIZES. THE STAR OF SVENDBORG IS FUN TO USE AS A GIFT BOX, OR EVEN AS A BALL FOR JUGGLING! THE STAR OF NYBORG ISN'T STRICTLY ORIGAMI, BECAUSE I USE GLUE, BUT THE EFFECT IS JUST THE SAME.

Faaborg

★★★★★

Actual size

MATERIALS
8 x paper squares, measuring
  4 x 4in (100 x 100mm)

TOOLS
Bone folder

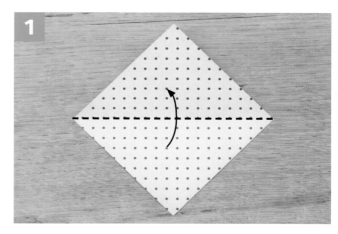

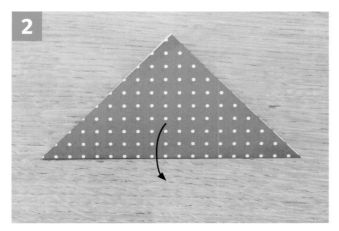

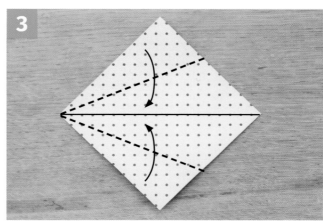

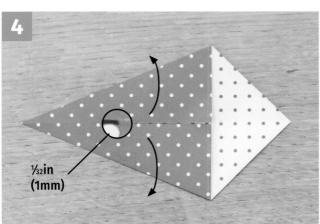

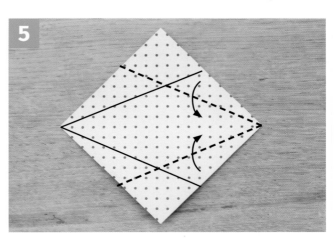

⅓₂in
(1mm)

1–2 With the paper square placed diagonally in front of you and right side down, fold in half horizontally to make a triangle. Open the square out again.

3–4 Fold the bottom left-hand side up to the middle fold and repeat with the top left-hand side to

make a kite shape, leaving approx. ⅓₂in (1mm) gap (approx. ⅟₁₆in/2mm if using a paper thicker than 80g) in the middle fold so there will be space for turning.

5 Open out and fold the other adjacent edges in the same way to form a kite shape pointing the other way.

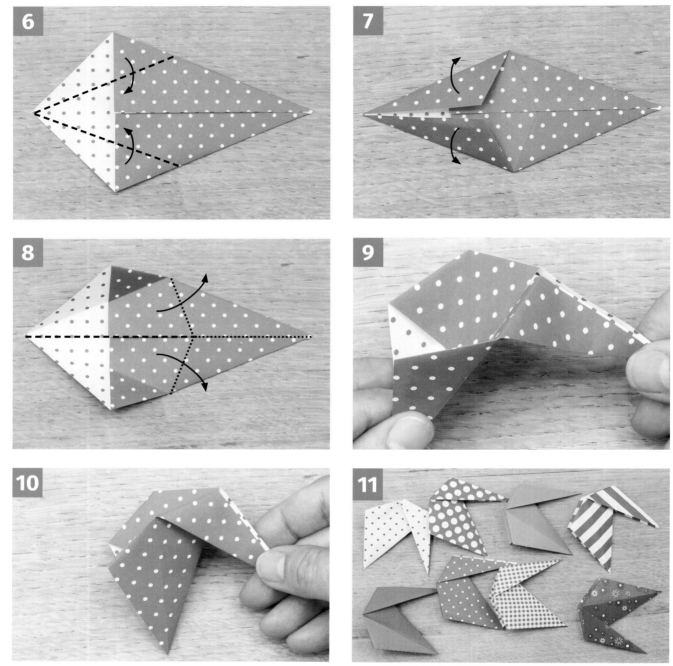

6–7 Fold the bottom left-hand edge of the shape up to the central fold, following the fold line already created, and repeat with the top left-hand edge. Open the shape out again.

8–11 Make an 'outside reverse fold' by folding the right-hand pointed end back and outwards at the diagonal fold lines and folding the central fold inwards. Fold seven more units in the same way.

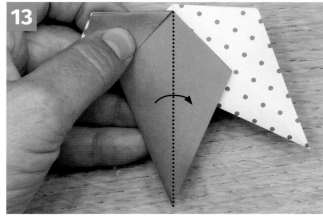

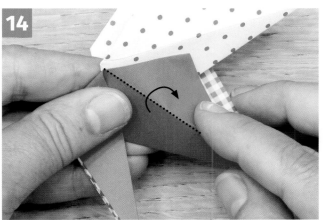

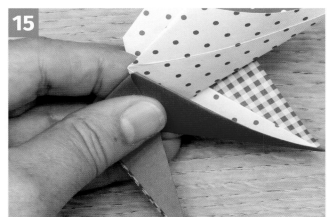

12–16 Insert the thin pointed triangle of one unit into the kite shape of another so you form a straight edge across the top. Fold the flap of the kite shape inwards over the inserted triangle so that it locks into a 'pocket'. Do the same on the other side.

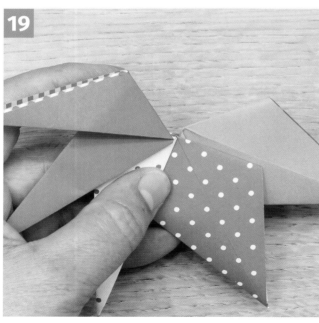

17–20 Carry on inserting the units into the star until the last unit is joined. Align the last kite shape so it fits around the first triangle and fold the flaps inwards.

Nyborg

★★★★★

Actual size

MATERIALS
13 x paper squares, measuring 4 x 4in
  (100 x 100mm)
Glue
Matching cotton thread

TOOLS
Scissors

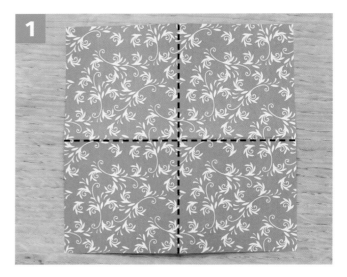

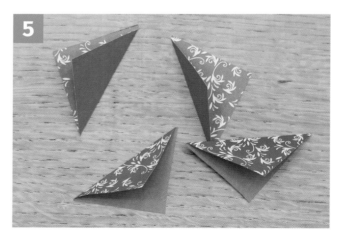

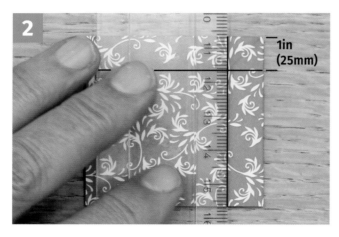

1 With the paper square placed right side up in front of you, fold it into quarters.

2–4 Measure and draw a line 1in (25mm) in from the two folded edges. Cut along these lines.

5 You will now have four smaller squares. Fold each of these small squares in half into triangles, as shown. Repeat Steps 1–5 twice to make 12 small triangles (you will only need 10).

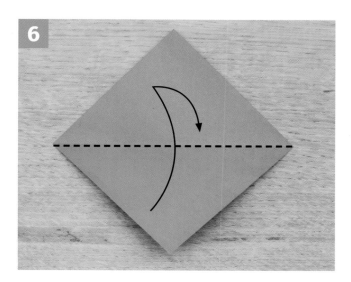

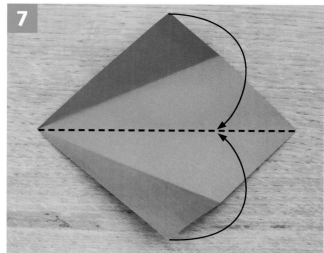

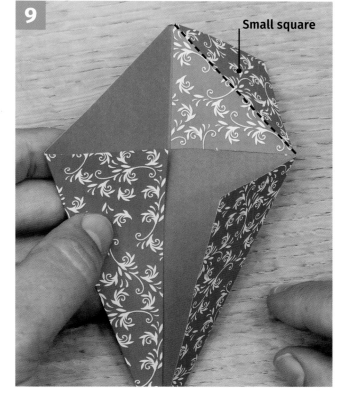

Small square

6 Now make ten kite shapes from the remaining squares, as follows. With right side down, fold a large square in half diagonally and unfold again.

7 With the square laying diagonally in front of you, fold the top left-hand edge down towards the crease you made in step 6 and the bottom left-hand edge up towards it. Repeat to make ten kite shapes.

8 Open one of your small triangles and apply a thin layer of glue to one half of the inside.

9 Fix the glued half of the square to the inside top of one of the kites, aligning its fold with the top edge of the kite, as shown.

★ **TIP** ★

Some types of paper don't work very well with glue. If you're having difficulty, try using ⅛in (3mm) double-sided tape instead.

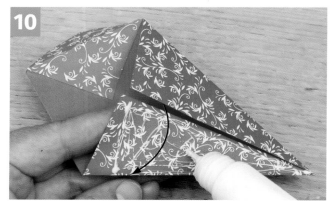

10 To form the kite shapes into cones, apply a thin layer of glue all over one long triangle, as shown.

11 Fold the other long triangle over the glued one, aligning the edges, and press firmly in place. Repeat for all ten kite shapes and leave to dry.

12 Apply a thin layer of glue to the inside flap of the small triangle.

13 Insert the glued flap into the top of a second cone and press in place to hinge two cones together.

14 Continue sticking together another three star cones until you have five joined together.

15 Make an identical star with the other five cones.

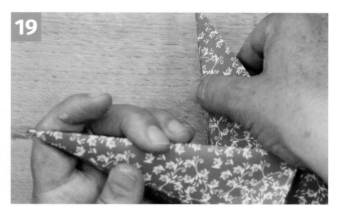

16 Cut a piece of thread long enough to hang your star with. Apply a thin line of glue down the centre of one of the star points

17 Place the thread on to the glued line.

18–20 Apply glue all over the remaining star points then carefully glue the two halves together, sandwiching the thread between two points. Take care to align the edges and match the tips.

Svendborg

★ ★ ★ ★ ★

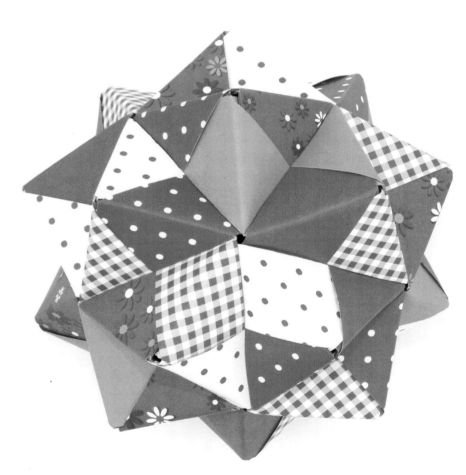

Actual size

MATERIALS
30 x paper squares in different
   patterns/colours, measuring 4 x 4in
   (100 x 100mm)

TOOLS
Bone folder

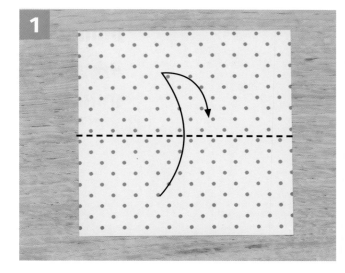

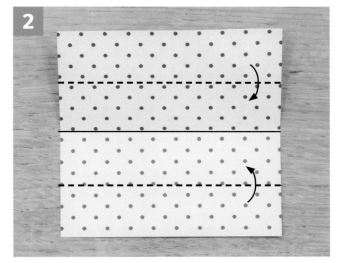

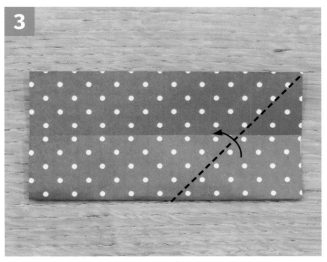

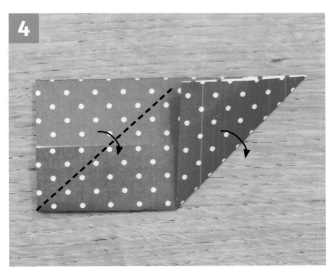

1–2 With the paper square placed right side down, fold in half horizontally to make a rectangle then open out and fold both edges in to meet at the centre fold.

3–4 Fold the bottom right-hand corner up so that the side edge meets the top edge to make a triangle. Repeat on the other side.

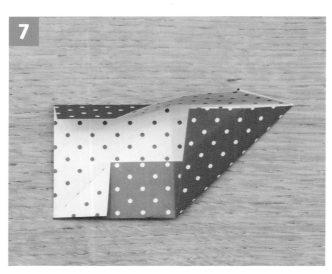

5–7 Open out the first triangle then fold a small triangle in the corner of the top flap. Repeat at the other end.

8 Open out the shape and fold the bottom triangle under the top flap. Turn the top small triangle inwards.

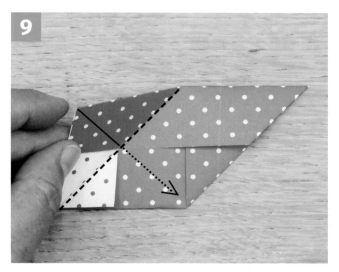

9–12 Repeat at the other end.

13–16 Fold the unit in half so the right-hand point comes over to the left side. Use a bone folder to help make the fold if you like. Fold back the top point to line up with the side of the shape as shown. Turn over and repeat with the other point. Make 29 more units.

17–22 Join three units together by inserting the point of one unit (A) into the 'pocket' of another (B). Then insert the point of a third unit (C) into the pocket of A. Then, insert the point of (B) into the pocket of (C). You may have to bend the shape a little to ease it in. This makes your first pyramid.

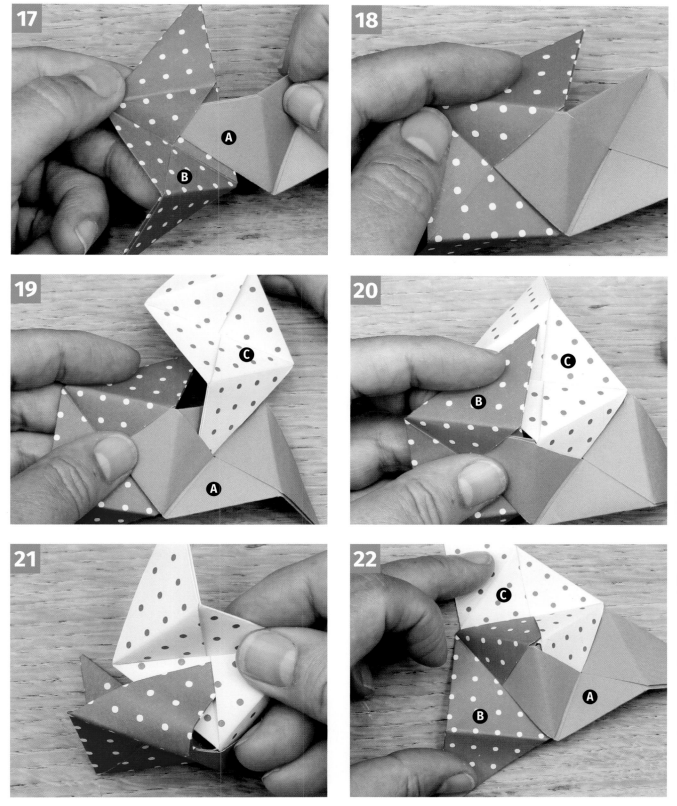

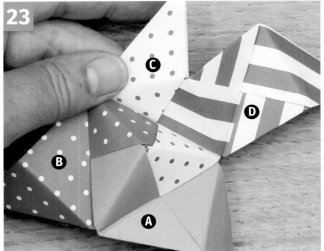

23–26 Carry on with the next pyramid by inserting the point of another single unit (D) into the pocket of (C). Insert another unit into (D) and continue around the shape with three more units to form a five-pointed pyramid.

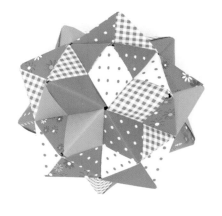

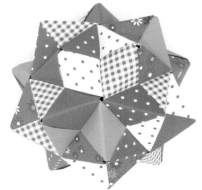

27–29 Continue like this until all units are connected. Close the shape up with the last point.

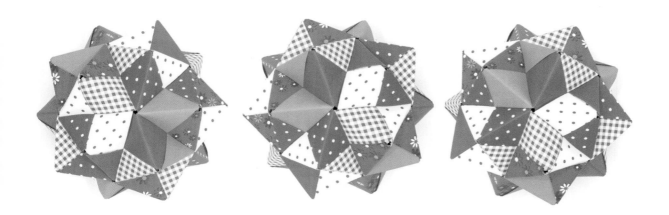

Kirigami Stars

KIRIGAMI IS THE ART OF FOLDING AND CUTTING PAPER. IT IS A WONDERFUL TECHNIQUE FOR CREATING PAPER STARS, AS NO TWO WILL BE EXACTLY ALIKE AND IT IS VERY EASY TO VARY THEM. THE BASIC TECHNIQUE IS USED FOR THE KOLDING STAR. TRY COMBINING ARTWORK FROM OLD BOOKS AND MAGAZINES WITH PLAIN-COLOURED PAPER, AS THIS CAN BE VERY EFFECTIVE. FINE PATTERNS ARE CUT FOR THE TØNDER STAR, WHICH CAN BE PLAITED TOGETHER OR COMBINED WITH KOLDING. VIBORG LOOKS DIFFICULT TO CREATE, BUT THE METHOD IS STRAIGHTFORWARD.

Kolding

★★★★★

Actual size

MATERIALS
3 x paper square, measuring 4 x 4in
  (100 x 100mm)
Glue

TOOLS
Scissors

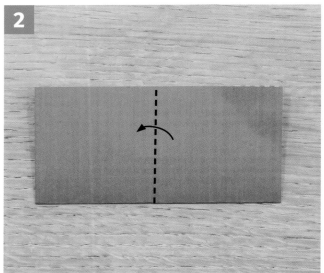

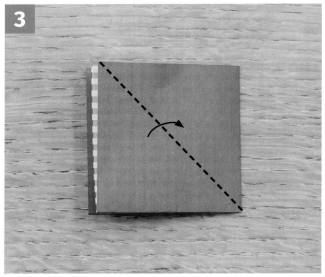

1 With the paper square placed right side down, fold in half vertically to make a rectangle.

2 Then fold the rectangle in half horizontally to make a quarter square.

3–4 Fold the bottom left-hand corner upwards diagonally into a triangle.

5 Turn it over and fold the bottom right-hand corner upwards to match.

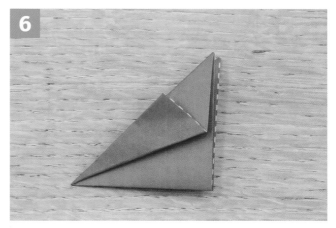

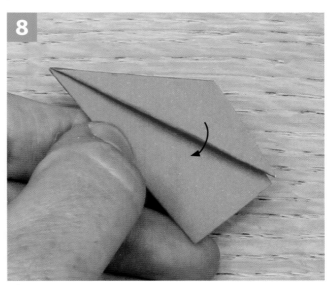

6 With the right angle at the bottom right-hand corner, fold the top flap upwards to meet the diagonal edge to the side.

7 Cut the corner as shown. The angle can be varied from star to star.

8 Fold the top flap back.

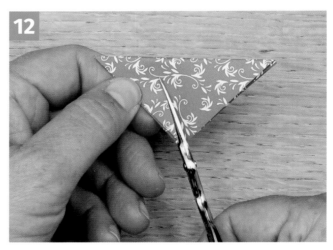

9–10 Cut the bottom corner as shown so that it matches the top.

11 Open out the star.

12–14 Choose your preferred paper and make two more stars (or as many as you like) in differing sizes to the first star. Vary the length of the points too, if you wish.

15–19 Rectangular paper can be cut in the same way. Here I have taken pages from an old book to create an interesting effect.

20–24 Layer your stars, joining them to each other with several tiny dabs of glue so that the paper doesn't bulge.

★ TIP ★

Some stars may need a little help to flatten them. If so, try pressing them in a book.

Tønder

★ ★ ★ ★ ★

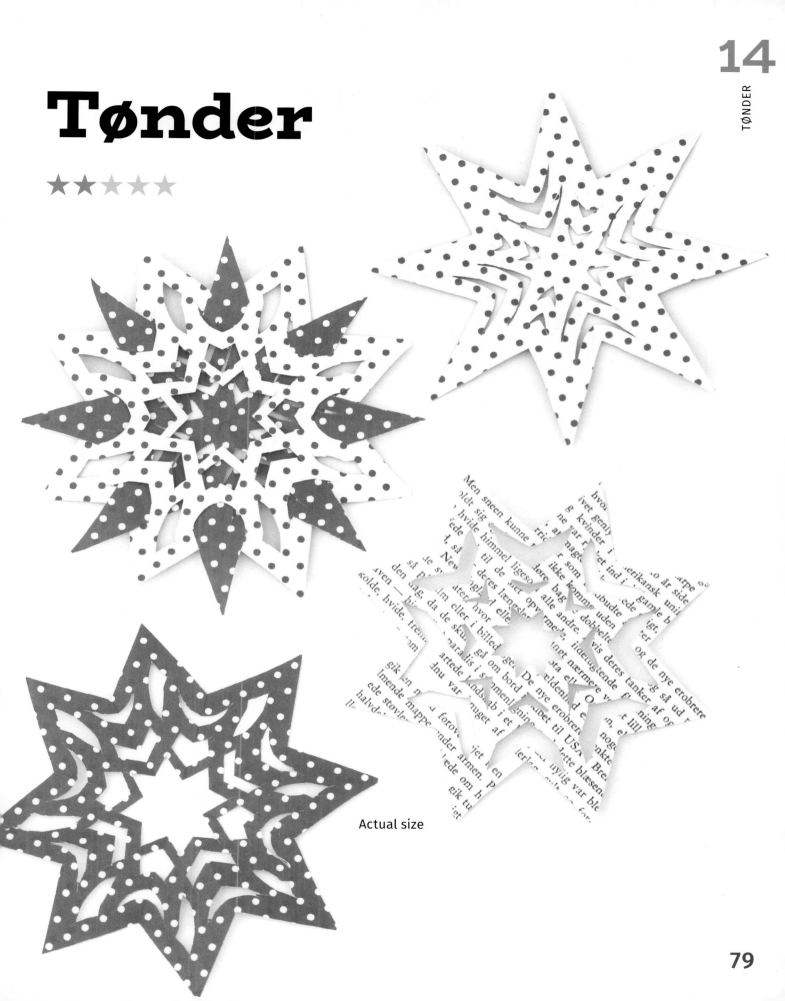

Actual size

MATERIALS
2 x paper squares, measuring
4 x 4in (100 x 100mm)

TOOLS
Scissors

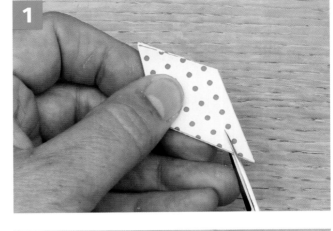

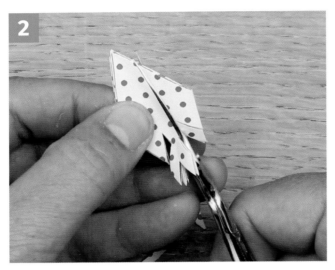

1–4 First make Star 13, Kolding, by following Steps 1–11 on pages 74–76. Then, using a pair of sharp-pointed scissors, cut out shapes in and up from the sides, making sure that the cutting lines cross so that you remove sections of paper. Small variations in the length of the cuts will make a big difference to the end result. Cut a triangle shape at the central point to create an open star in the middle.

5–7 Repeat Steps 1–4 to make two more stars.

8–10 Weave them together, using a little glue to keep them attached.

★ **TIP** ★

These stars also look beautiful when combined with the Kolding star on page 73.

81

Viborg

Actual size

MATERIALS
2 x paper squares, measuring
 4 x 4in (100 x 100mm)

TOOLS
Scissors

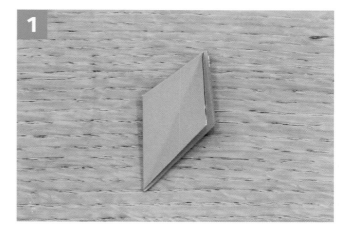

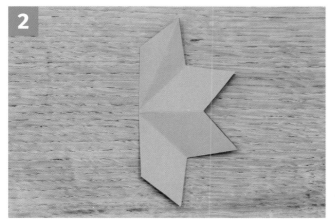

1–2 First make the Kolding star by following Steps 1–11 on pages 74–76. Open it out and fold the star in half.

3 Cut a small upwards half-crescent shape for the nose about ¾in (20mm) below the middle point.

4 Cut a smaller, half-bow shape for the upper lip, then cut a small triangle to form the bottom lip – this should be about the same distance down as the upper lip thickness.

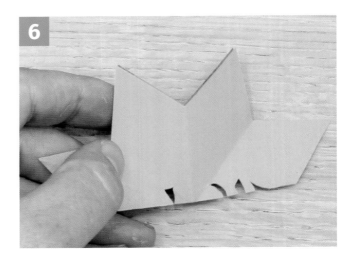

5 Make a long curved cut just above the middle point to form the upper eyeline (A).

6 At the end of the line cut a small triangle shape for the eye.

7 Cut another triangle shape close to the fold line, creating an eyeball shape between them. You can add another curved line above to create an eyebrow shape.

8–11 Fold each point in half and cut narrow triangles from both sides. Unfold.

12–15 Experiment with cutting out other shapes. For closed shapes, prick a hole in the middle (B) with scissors and cut lines to each corner (B–C, B–D, B–E) – this will make enough space for the scissors to cut out the shape.

Quilling Stars

PAPER QUILLING IS A TECHNIQUE THAT HAS EXISTED SINCE THE RENAISSANCE. INTRICATE PATTERNS CAN BE MADE USING IT. I HAVE ONLY BEEN QUILLING FOR FIVE YEARS, BUT I'M ENTHRALLED WITH IT, AND HAVE DEVELOPED A SYSTEM THAT MAKES IT VERY EASY TO QUILL PAPER STARS. SØNDERBORG IS A DELICATE STAR THAT IS PERFECT AS A CHRISTMAS DECORATION. THE FLENSBORG INCORPORATES A MIRROR IMAGE PATTERN, MAKING IT ESPECIALLY HARMONIOUS. HAMBURG SHOWS JUST HOW BEAUTIFUL REPEATED PATTERNS CAN BE IN THESE STARS.

Sønderborg

★★★★★

Actual size

MATERIALS

10 x paper strips, measuring
17¾ x ³⁄₁₆in (450 x 5mm)
1 x paper strip, measuring
17¾ x ⅛in (450 x 3mm)
Glue
⅛in (3mm) double-sided
tape

TOOLS

Quilling pen
Tweezers
Measuring board
Pins
Bone folder (optional)

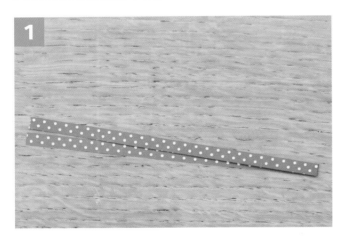

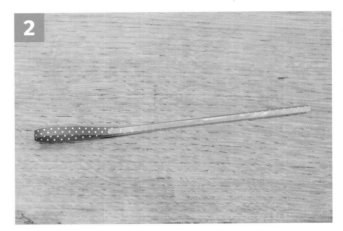

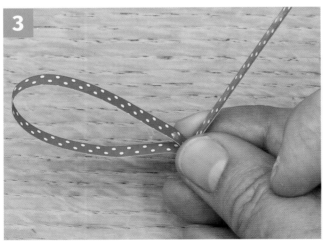

1 Fold a ³⁄₁₆in (5mm) paper strip in half as shown, then tear in half. Repeat with two other strips.

2–4 Make six Loop B units (see page 131 for instructions).

5 Press each one flat and mark ¾in (20mm) from one end with a fingernail or a bone folder.

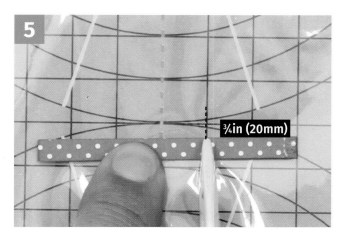

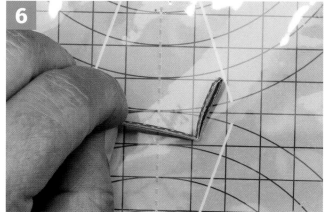

¾in (20mm)

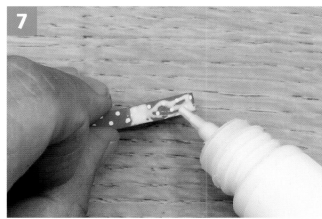

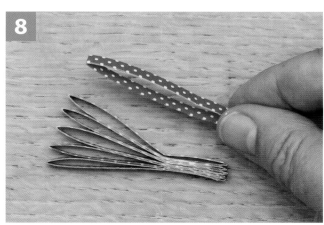

6 Fold backwards and forwards at the point you have marked.

7 Apply a small amount of glue to the section below the ¾in (20mm) mark.

8–10 Join the glued part of the units together one by one, then join the first and last units together to make a star shape.

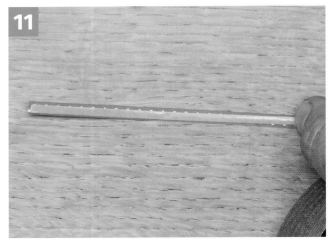

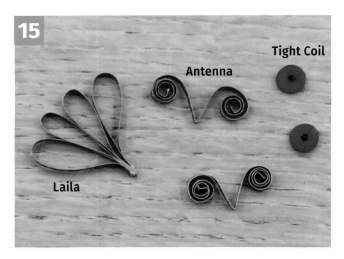

Tight Coil

Antenna

Laila

11–14 To reinforce the star, stick double-sided tape to a ³⁄₁₆in (5mm) paper strip and fasten it around the perimeter of the star. Make sure the paper is stuck all the way to the bottom of each 'valley'. This may skew the star – if so, gently straighten it again.

15 Now make the shapes to fill the units. Using the ³⁄₁₆in (5mm) strips, fold six 9in (225mm) Laila shapes (see page 136) and twelve 4½in (112mm) Antenna shapes (see page 137). Using the ⅛in (3mm) paper strip, make two 9in (225mm) Tight Coils (see page 135).

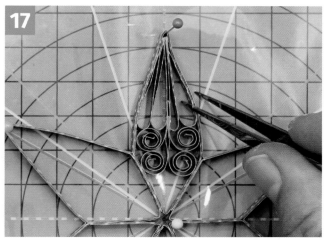

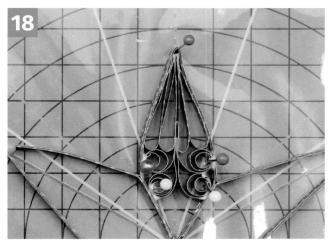

16–18 Fix the star to the measuring board with pins, using the pink lines as a guide. Glue one Laila into position. Stick two Antenna shapes together and place the joined-together strip in the middle of one of the Laila shapes. Glue in all the places where the shapes touch. Use a pair of tweezers or pins to hold the shapes until the glue is dry. Remember to remove any pins before they get stuck!

19–20 Finally, take the two Tight Coils and glue one on each side of the centre.

Flensborg

★★★★☆

Actual size

MATERIALS
29 x paper strips,
  measuring 17¾ x ³⁄₁₆in
  (450 x 5mm)
8 x paper strips,
  measuring 17¾ x ⅛in
  (450 x 3mm)
Glue
⅛in (3mm) double-sided
  tape

TOOLS
Quilling pen
Tweezers
Measuring board
Pins
Bone folder (optional)

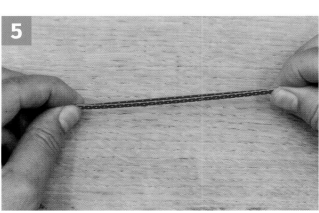

1–4 With the ³⁄₁₆in (5mm) paper strips, make six
Loop A units (see page 131 for instructions).

5 Press each one flat.

★ TIP ★
Make Star 16, Sønderborg, before you attempt this.

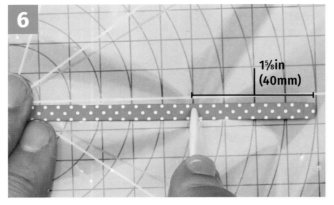

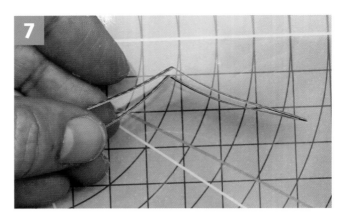

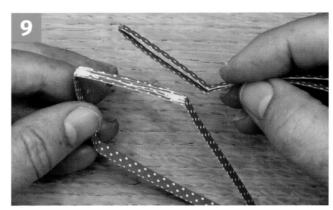

6 Mark 1⅝in (40mm) from one end with a fingernail or a bone folder.

7 Fold backwards and forwards at the point you have marked.

8–11 Apply a small amount of glue to the section below the 1⅝in (40mm) mark. Join the glued part of the units together one by one, then join the first and last units together to make a star shape.

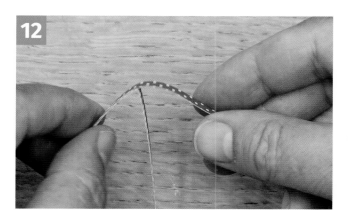

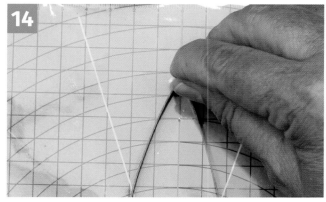

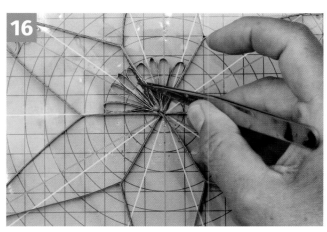

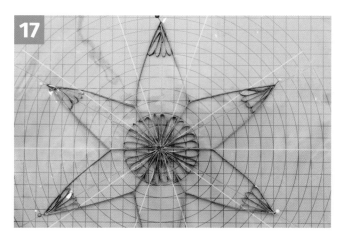

12–13 To reinforce the star, stick double-sided tape to two of the ³⁄₁₆in (5mm) paper strips and fasten them around the perimeter of the star. Make sure the paper is stuck all the way to the bottom of each 'valley'. This may skew the star – if so, gently straighten it again.

14 Pin the star on the measuring board, using the pink ⅛th sector lines.

15 Now make the shapes to fill the star. Fold 18 Laila shapes (see page 136) and 24 Antenna shapes (see page 137). Apply glue to one Laila.

16–17 Place one Laila inside each pointed tip of the star and one at the centre.

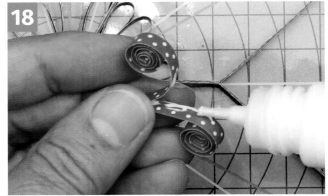

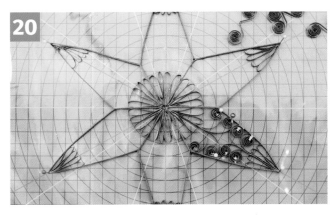

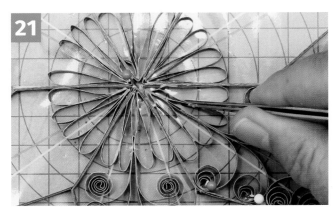

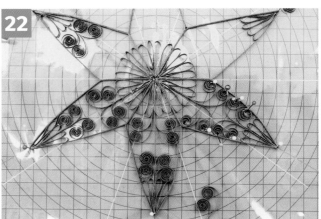

18–19 Stick two Antenna shapes together and place the joined-together strip in the middle of one Laila.

20 Continue sticking together the rest of the shapes in the same way. Glue in all the places where they touch, making especially sure that the coils of the Antenna shapes are glued to the sides of the star. Use tweezers or pins to hold the shapes until the glue is dry.

21–23 Roll six Tight Coils using the ⅛in (3mm) paper strips and glue them on both sides. Position as shown in the photograph on page 92. Lastly, glue the remaining six Lailas into each 'valley'.

★ TIP ★

The sides of the Laila loops can be glued together to make the star stronger.

Hamburg

★★★★★

Actual size

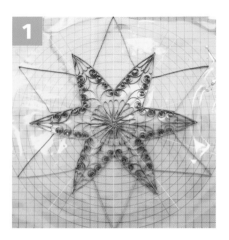

MATERIALS
55 x paper strips, measuring
   17¾ x ³⁄₁₆in (450 x 5mm)
8 x paper strips, measuring
   17¾ x ⅛in (450 x 3mm)
Glue
⅛in (3mm) double-sided
   tape

TOOLS
Quilling pen
Tweezers
Measuring board (you will
   need to extend the lines)
Pins
Bone folder (optional)

1 Begin by making Flensborg (see page 92) but leave out the Laila shapes between the points. Make six extra Loop A units (see page 131) and glue them to the star.

2 Fill the units with Laila and Antenna shapes, as for Flensborg.

3–4 Reinforce the perimeter of the star with double-sided tape on a strip of paper, making sure the strip reaches right down into the bottom of the 'valleys'.

★ TIP ★
The sides of the Laila loops can be glued together to make the star stronger.

Galaxy Comb-Quilling Stars

THE GALAXY STARS ARE MY LATEST DESIGNS. THEY ARE SO SIMPLE TO MAKE, AND I LOVE THE GRAPHIC EFFECT THAT IS CREATED BY ALL THE DIFFERENT LINES. THE SMALL STARS LOOK WONDERFUL ON THE CHRISTMAS TREE. THEY CAN BE MADE IN ANY COLOUR YOU LIKE; IT'S EVEN POSSIBLE TO GIVE EACH POINT ITS OWN COLOUR. THE LARGER STARS HAVE ENOUGH IMPACT TO BE HUNG ALONE, BUT PERSONALLY I THINK THEY LOOK THEIR BEST IN CLUSTERS.

Meissa

★★☆☆☆

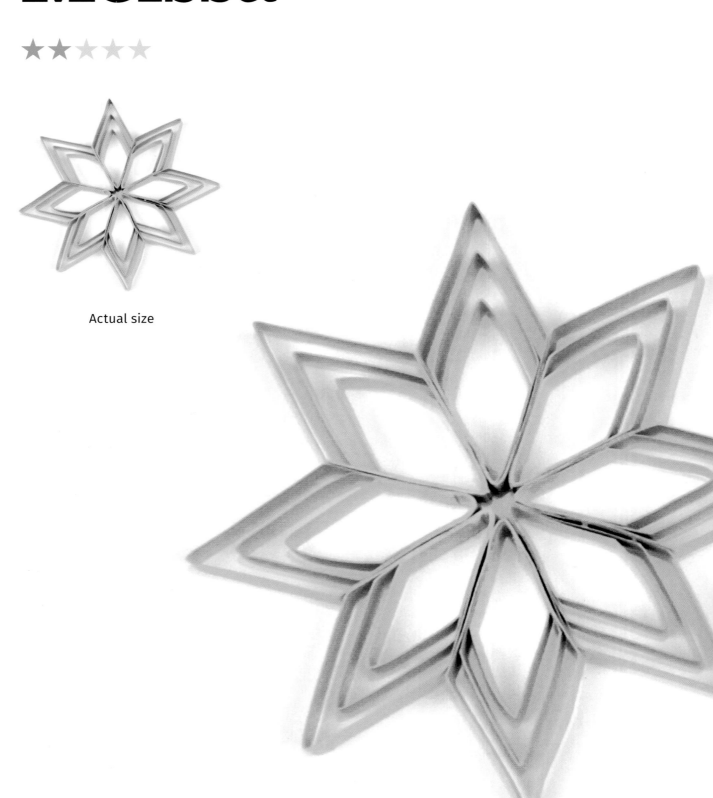

Actual size

MATERIALS
3 x paper strips, measuring
  17¾ x ³⁄₁₆in (450 x 5mm)
Glue

TOOLS
Comb
Scissors
Pins
Measuring board

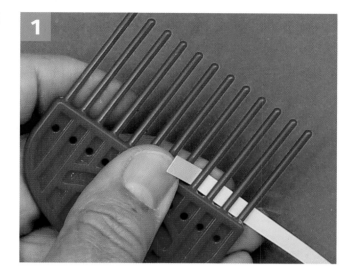

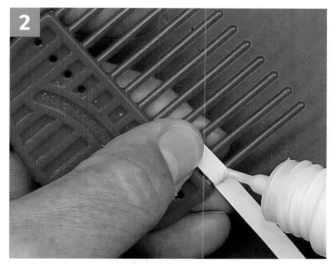

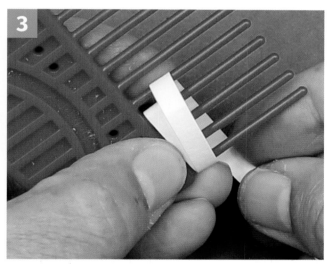

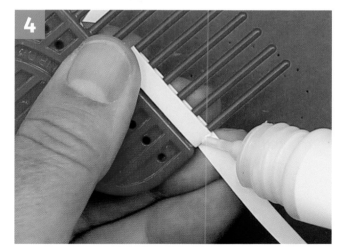

1 Hold the comb in one hand. Take one strip and put the end under the comb and up after four teeth.

2 Fold the paper so that its tip reaches the start of the comb. Put a dab of glue at the end of the strip.

3 Fold the long end of the paper strip over the top of the comb and down after the next tooth along the comb.

4 Add another dab of glue at the start of the comb. Continue to wind from side to side, increasing the size of the folds each time by using the next tooth on the comb. Glue at the side edge after each fold.

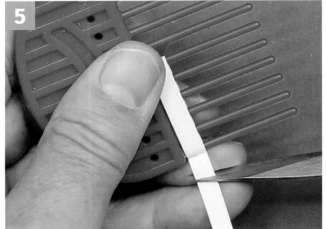

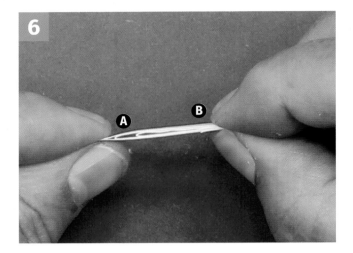

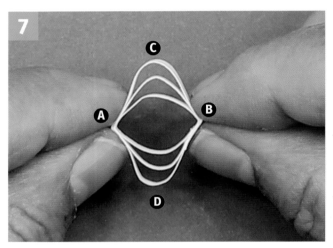

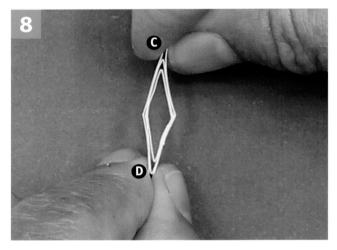

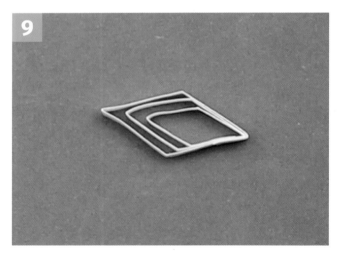

5 Repeat to make three loops. Make sure you don't wind the paper tightly, otherwise you will find it difficult to remove from the comb. Also, take care to ensure the strips are lying straight. Cut the strip and glue, then slide it off the comb. Repeat the process using the rest of the strip – you should be able to make three star units from it.

6 Press the strip of paper flat and make sure the ends A and B are sharply folded.

7 Gently press A and B towards each other, taking care that C and D are opposite each other.

8–9 Press the ends C and D flat to form a small diamond. Repeat Steps 1–9 to make the other seven units.

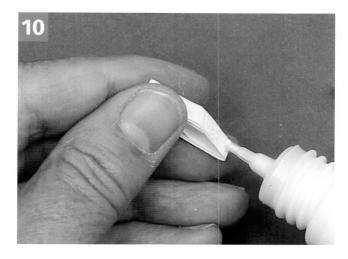

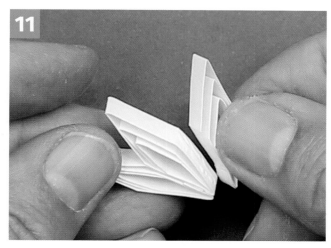

10 Apply a small amount of glue to the bottom half of the diamond.

11 Glue four units together at C-A and D-A. Repeat with the other four units.

12–13 Pin and glue the two four-unit parts using the green ⅛th lines on the measuring board. Make sure there is a little space left at the centre. Remove the star from the measuring board.

14 Thread a length of cotton through the middle.

Riga

★★★★★

Actual size

MATERIALS
8 x paper strips, measuring
  17¾ x ³⁄₁₆in (450 x 5mm)
Glue

TOOLS
Comb
Scissors
Pins
Measuring board

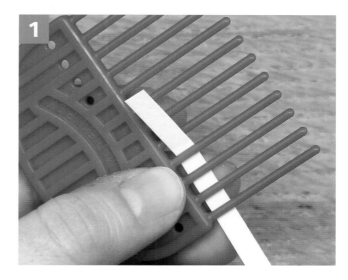

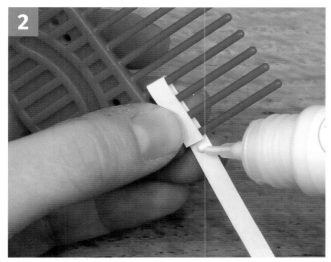

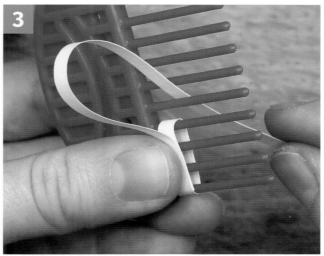

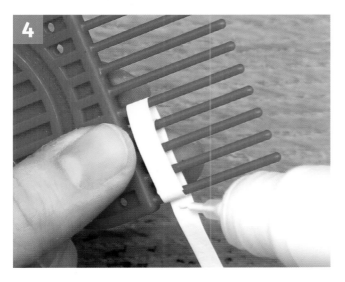

1 Hold the comb in one hand. Take one strip and put the end under the comb and up after four teeth.

2 Fold the paper so that the end reaches the start of the comb. Put a small dab of glue at the end of the strip

3 Fold the long end of the paper strip over the top of the comb and down behind the next tooth along.

4 Add another dab of glue at the start of the comb.

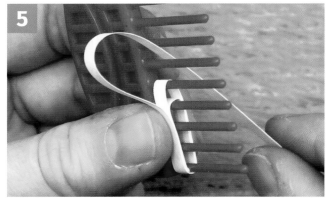

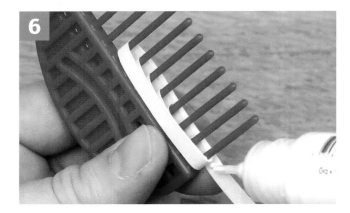

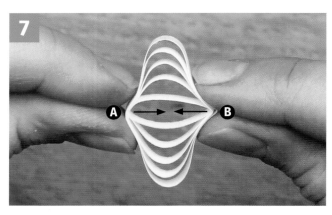

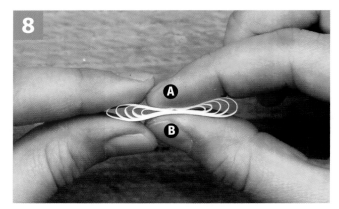

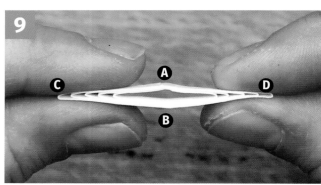

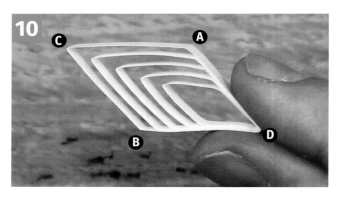

5 Continue to wind from side to side, increasing the size of the folds each time by using the next tooth on the comb. Glue at the side edge after each fold.

6 Do this for five rounds. Make sure you don't wind the paper tightly, otherwise you will find it difficult to remove from the comb. Also, take care to ensure the strips are lying straight. Cut the strip and glue, then slide it off the comb. Press the strip of paper flat and make the ends A and B sharp.

7 Gently press A and B towards each other, taking care that A and B are on top of each other.

8 Turn the unit and press A and B flat. It can be difficult because there are five layers of paper. If you find it impossible – you might have used too much glue!

9–10 Press the ends C and D flat. Repeat Steps 1–9 to make the other seven units.

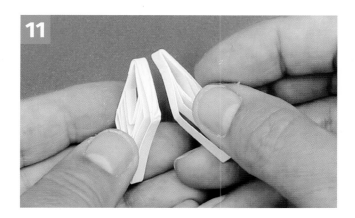

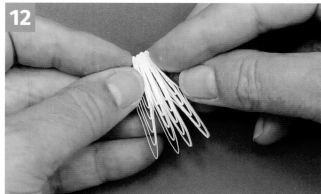

11–12 Apply a small amount of glue to the bottom half of the diamond. Glue four units together at B-C and B-D. Repeat with the other four units.

13–14 Pin and glue the two four-unit parts using the green ⅛th lines on the measuring board. Make sure there is a little space left at the centre.

15 Remove the star from the measuring board and thread a length of cotton through the middle.

★ **TIP** ★

You can make a 12-pointed star in the same way. Just turn the measuring board over and follow the pink and white lines.

Lyra

★★★★★

Actual size

MATERIALS
16 x paper strips, measuring
17¾ x 3⁄16in (450 x 5mm)
Glue

TOOLS
Comb
Scissors
Pins
Measuring board

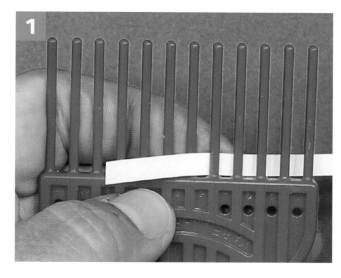

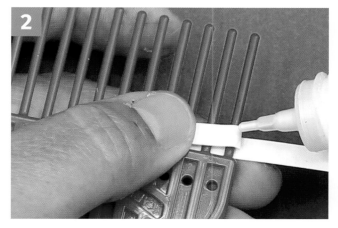

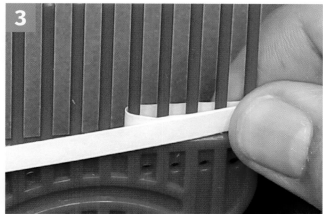

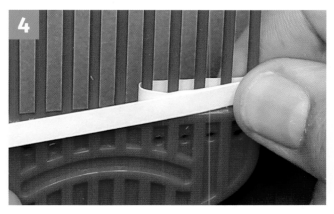

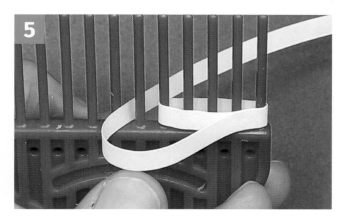

1 Hold the comb in one hand. Take one strip and put the end under the comb and up after five teeth.

2 Fold the paper so that the end reaches the start of the comb. Put a small dab of glue at the end of the strip.

3–4 Fold the long end of the paper strip over the top of the comb and down after the next tooth along.

5 Add another dab of glue at the start of the comb.

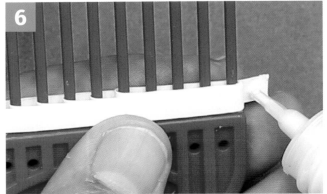

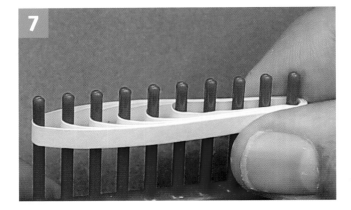

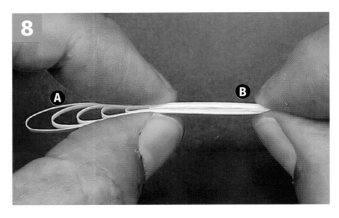

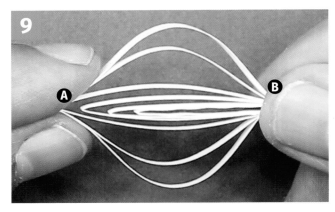

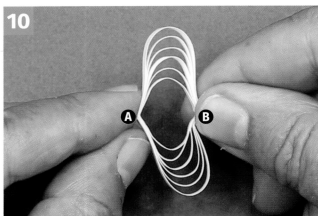

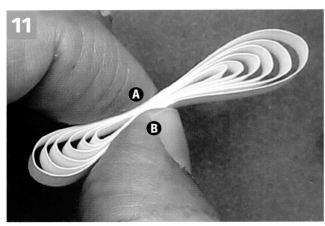

6 Continue to wind from side to side, increasing the size of the folds each time by using the next tooth on the comb. Glue at the side edge after each fold.

7 Repeat for six rounds. Make sure you don't wind the paper tightly, otherwise you will find it difficult to remove from the comb. Also, take care to ensure the strips are lying straight. Cut the strip and glue, then slide it off the comb.

8 Repeat Steps 1–7 to make the other 15 units. Press the strip of paper flat and make the ends A and B sharp.

9–11 Gently press A and B towards each other, taking care that A and B are on top of each other. It can be difficult because there are six layers of paper. If you find it impossible – you may have used too much glue!

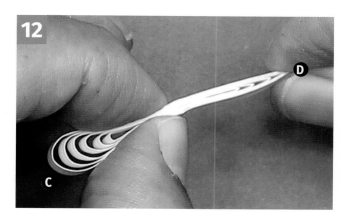

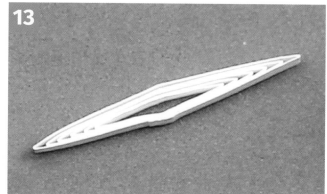

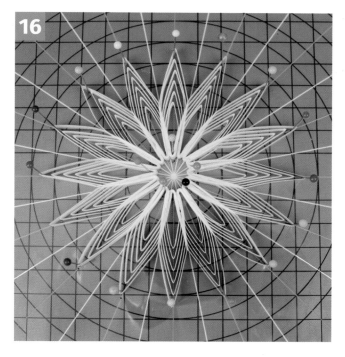

12–13 Press the ends C and D flat to form a small diamond. Press C and D towards each other to give the correct diamond shape. Repeat the process with the other 15 units.

14 Apply a small amount of glue to the bottom half of the diamond. Glue four units together at C-A and D-A. Repeat with the other 12 units.

15–16 Pin and glue the four four-unit parts onto the green and orange lines on the measuring board. Make sure there is a little space left at the centre. Remove the star from the measuring board and thread a length of cotton through the middle.

★ TIP ★

Make the Meissa star (see page 100) or Riga star (see page 104) first before attempting this one.

Curled Galaxy Stars

IT'S MAGICAL HOW THE APPEARANCE OF A STAR CAN BE
ALTERED BY A LITTLE BIT OF CURLING. I FIND WORKING
TO ACHIEVE THE BEST BALANCE BETWEEN LINES AND
CURLS A FASCINATING ACTIVITY. VERY OFTEN I COME TO
THE CONCLUSION THAT LESS IS MORE! THIS TECHNIQUE
IS SO SIMPLE, BUT WITH IT YOU CAN CREATE LOTS OF
AMAZING STARS. I VERY MUCH HOPE YOU WILL MAKE
MANY VARIATIONS AND FIND YOUR OWN FAVOURITES.

Sirius

Actual size

MATERIALS
8 x paper strips, measuring
   17¾ x ³⁄₁₆in (450 x 5mm)
Glue

TOOLS
Quilling pen
Comb
Scissors
Pins
Measuring board

1–3 First make a Riga star with eight points (see pages 104–107). Hold the star firmly in your hand. Place the quilling pen at the top of the inner point. Hold it straight and roll it away from yourself (clockwise). Continue until all eight inner points have a curl.

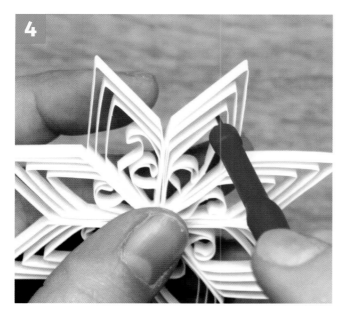

4–6 Now put the quilling pen in the next point above and try to roll in the other direction (anticlockwise). If you find this difficult you can flip the star around and roll clockwise.

Orion

Actual size

MATERIALS

16 x paper strips, measuring
  17¾ x ³⁄₁₆in (450 x 5mm)
Glue

TOOLS

Quilling pen
Comb
Scissors
Pins
Measuring board

1–3 First make a Lyra star with 16 points and six rounds (see pages 108–111). Hold the star firmly. Put the quilling pen at the top of the second innermost point and roll it away from yourself (clockwise). This gives a double effect. Repeat with the remaining 15 inner points.

★ TIP ★

Vary the design by curling every second point, curling anticlockwise as well, or leaving some of the star units uncurled.

Tania

Actual size

MATERIALS
32 x paper strips, measuring
  17¾ x ³⁄₁₆in (450 x 5mm)
Glue

TOOLS
Quilling pen
Comb
Scissors
Pins
Measuring board

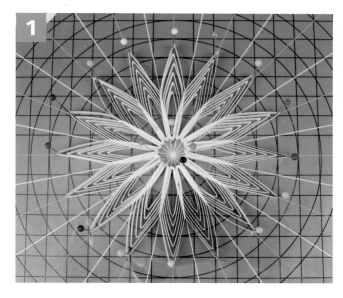

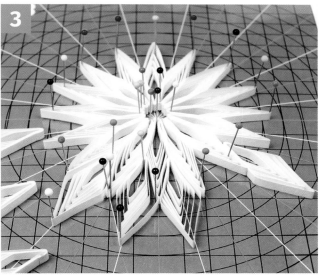

1 First make a Lyra star with 16 points and six rounds (see pages 108–111). Keep the star pinned to the measuring board.

2 Make 16 more star units. Glue and pin the units into place as shown, one by one, spreading the glue on the sides of each unit.

3 Put in pins at the corners to make sure that the glue makes contact.

4 Now create curls in the outer 16 units by repeating Steps 2–6 of Sirius (see pages 114–115).

Maribo

★★★★★

Actual size

MATERIALS
24 x paper strips, measuring
  17¾ x 3/16in (450 x 5mm)
Glue

TOOLS
Comb
Scissors
Pins
Measuring board

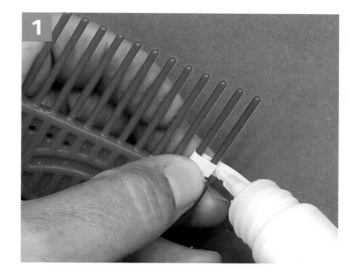

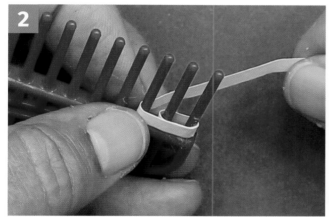

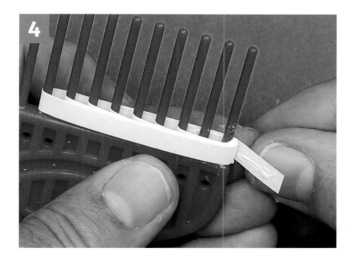

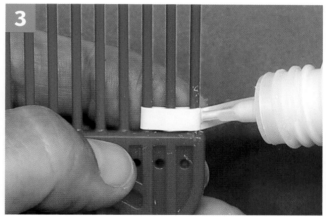

★ TIP ★
Try making Sirius (see page 113), Orion (see page 116) and Tania (see page 118) before this one.

1 Hold the comb in one hand. Take one strip and put the end under the comb and up after two teeth. Fold the paper so that it fits with the start of the comb. Put a small dab of glue and fold the long end of the paper strip over the top of the comb and down after the next tooth along. Add another dab of glue at the start of the comb.

2–4 Continue to wind from side to side, increasing the size of the folds each time by using the next tooth on the comb. Add another dab of glue at the start of the comb. Repeat for eight rounds. Make sure you don't wind the paper tightly, otherwise you will find it difficult to remove from the comb. Also, take care to ensure the strips are lying straight.

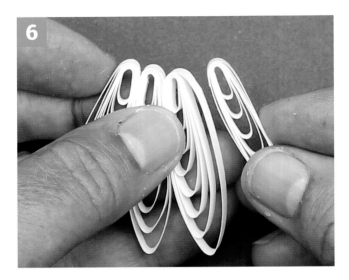

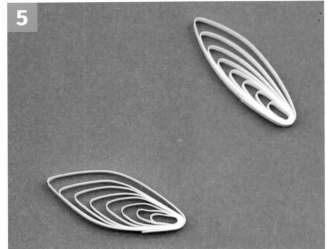

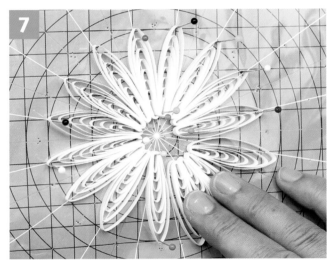

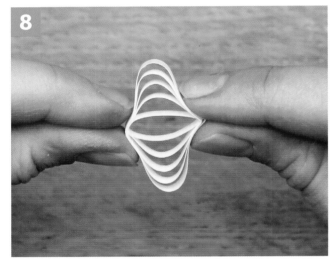

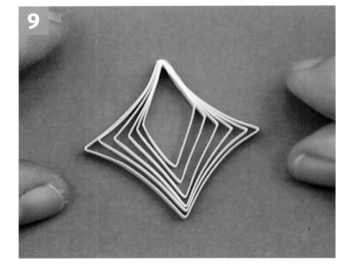

5 Slide the paper off the comb. Repeat Steps 1–5 to make the other 15 units.

6 Glue four units together. Note: only glue ⅜in (10mm) from the base.

7 Place them on your measuring board and pin so the unit fits between the green and orange lines and the top of the unit matches the white lines. Continue in this way until they have all been glued and pinned.

8 Now make eight star units with six rounds over five teeth, just like those for Riga (see pages 104–107). Give the corners a rounded shape so that they fit between the flower petals.

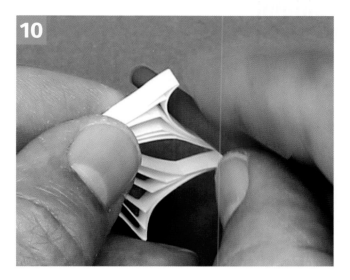

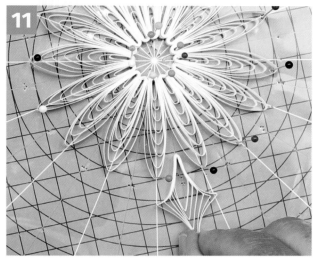

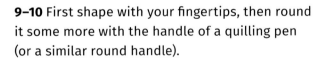

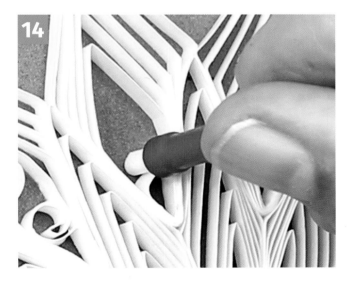

9–10 First shape with your fingertips, then round it some more with the handle of a quilling pen (or a similar round handle).

11–12 Glue and pin the eight units, one by one, in between the star points.

13–14 Now create curls for the inner 16 units by repeating Steps 2–6 of Sirius (see pages 114–115). Then repeat the process for the outer eight units.

Tools and materials

I use my own brand of tools and materials (available to purchase through my website – see page 141 for details); however, it is possible to make your own measuring board, quilling comb and pen. You will find instructions here on how to do so. The other tools and materials should all be easy to source through your local craft suppliers or online.

Quilling comb

MATERIALS
Template on page 138
12 x paper strips measuring 1 x 2¾in
   (25 x 70mm)
1 x paper strip measuring 1 x 11in
   (25 x 280mm)
Strong white glue
12 x wooden cocktail sticks

TOOLS
Scissors

Note: The paper used here is 120g. If you use a thinner paper the strips must be longer, because it is important that the width between the comb teeth is the same as used in the book.

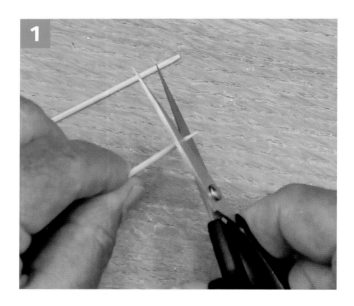

1 Cut off one of the pointed ends of each stick.

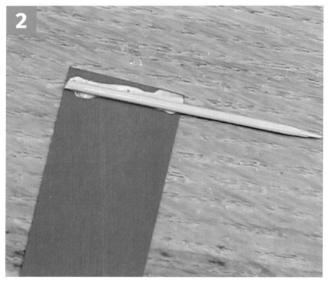

2 Glue the blunt end of the stick to the short end of the paper and let it dry.

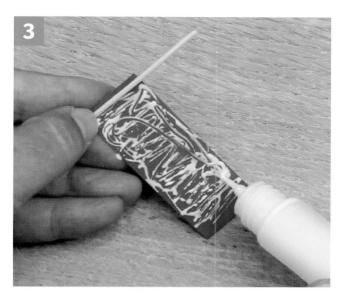

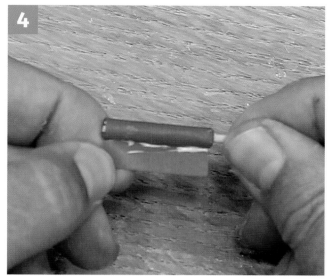

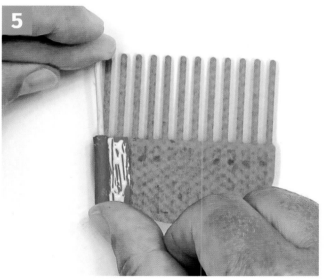

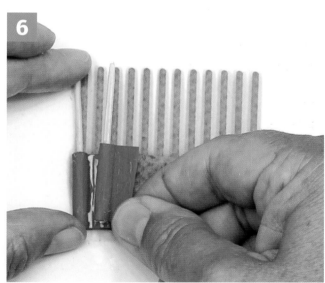

3 Spread glue over the rest of the paper.

4 Now roll the paper tightly but leave about ⅜in (10mm) at the end. This will be the base for the next stick. Repeat 11 more times.

5 Check against the template on page 138 that each roll is the correct width, with the wooden sticks the same distance apart as on the template. Note that the teeth don't have to be this long.

6–7 Now glue all the sticks together.

7

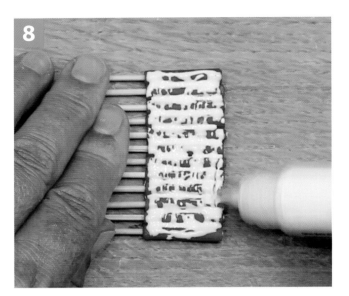

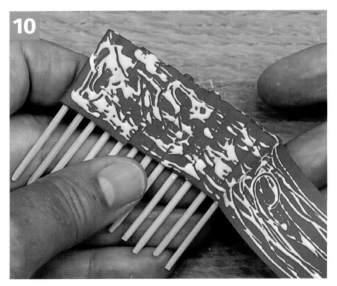

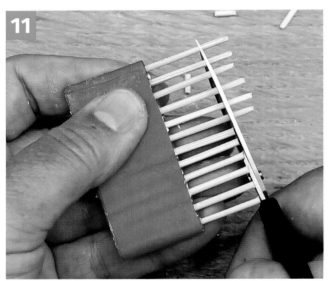

8 Spread glue all over the upper side.

9 Place the long paper strip on top.

10 Spread glue on the long strip and fold it tightly around.

11 Cut off the wooden sticks to a length of ¾in (20mm). (It is easiest to work with this length.) Let your comb dry completely before you start to use it – a minimum of three hours, depending on which glue, and how much, you have used; it will be spoiled if you start to quill right away when the paper is still wet.

Quilling pen

MATERIALS
1 x wooden cocktail stick
1 x paper strip measuring
   1 x 2¾–4in (25 x 70–100mm)
Glue

TOOLS
Scissors

★ **TIP** ★

*If you prefer to make the handle
thicker, simply wind on more paper.*

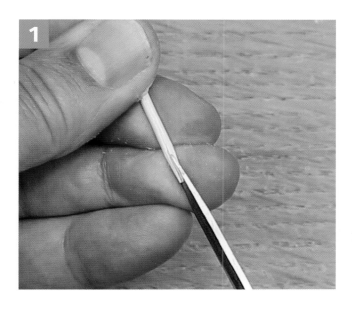

1 Cut a slot in the tip of the stick.

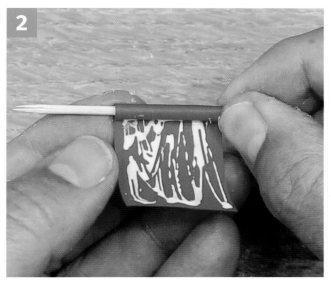

2 Spread glue on the paper strip and wind it tightly
around the middle of the stick to complete your
quilling pen.

Measuring boards

MATERIALS
Templates on page 139–140
Photocopier paper
Plastic bag
Corrugated cardboard, cork or foam
  to match the size of the templates
Glue

TOOLS
Scissors
Colour photocopier

Make your own measuring board by colour photocopying the templates at actual size. Place them in a clear plastic bag. This is important so you don't glue the stars to the paper. For a backing mat, you can use corrugated cardboard, cork or foam – it doesn't matter as long as it's possible to insert pins and remove them again.

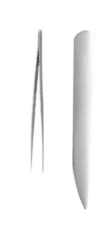

Tweezers

These can be used instead of pins to hold the stars in place on the measuring board. They are also useful for positioning the different shapes within the units.

Bone folder

This tool is particularly helpful when making origami stars and other folded components.

Scissors

Medium-sized, sharp-pointed scissors are the most useful type to have to hand.

Craft knife and blades

Any craft knife will be suitable.

Cutting mat

The cutting mat (or board) should be used when you cut with a craft knife. The grid on the mat is also useful for measuring.

Thread

This is used to tie folded star parts together – it can be a sewing thread of any kind. It's best if the colour of the thread matches the paper you are using.

Ruler

It is best to use a non-slip metal ruler when you are working with a craft knife – that way you get a fine, straight cut.

Paper strips

The strips used in these projects are made from 115g to 125g paper. These are the best weights for quilling. Thinner paper is difficult to work with.

Origami and folding paper

For the origami stars, 80g paper has been used, but for some stars it's possible to use paper that weighs up to 125g, or even 190g. The larger the star, the thicker the paper required.

129

Cutting paper

Thin paper is easiest to cut, especially if it's folded many times. But it's great to work with all kinds of paper, including printed sheets, newspaper, handmade paper or metallic-finish paper. It's a good idea to start a collection, so you always have plenty of choice.

Glue

I always use my own brand of glue (see page 141 for mailorder details). If you can't get hold of this, use a white glue that dries fast and is not too wet. Glue is also used to stiffen the stars, so it must be one that dries hard.

Pins

You will need thin pins to stick into the measuring board and hold your stars in place. A good-sized head on the pins makes them easier to use.

⅛in (3mm) double-sided tape

This tape is readily available and simple to work with. Make sure you buy the very thin type that tears easily.

Techniques

Some of the techniques used in this book are well known, but others I have developed to create unique stars. For instance, the Laila shape (page 136) is not really a quilling technique, it's more akin to folding, but I only use it for quilled stars. The techniques shown here can be used for all kinds of quilling projects.

Guide to symbols

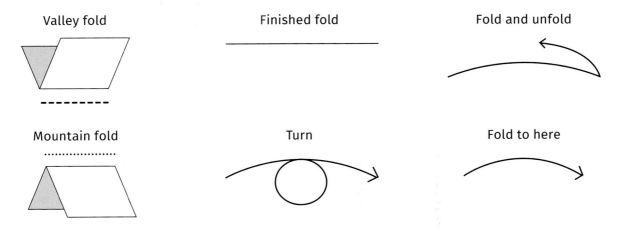

Valley fold

Finished fold

Fold and unfold

Mountain fold

Turn

Fold to here

Basic units

All the stars are constructed from basic units that are glued together.

Loops A & B

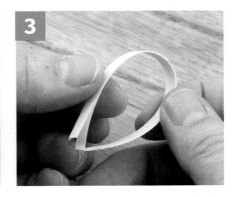

1 Take one strip of paper measuring 17½in (450mm) for a Loop A unit or 8⅞in (225mm) for a Loop B unit and fold in half.

2 Form one half of the strip into a loop. On the other half, attach a length of ⅛in (3mm) double-sided tape.

3 Take the side with the double-sided tape up and over the loop to form a double-layered loop. It can then be pressed flat and folded in different ways as per the instructions in the projects.

Galaxy comb quilling

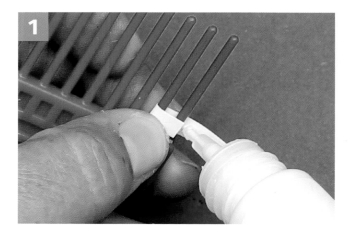

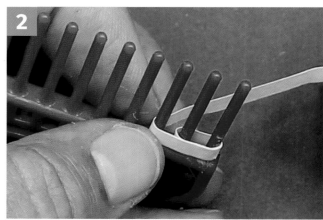

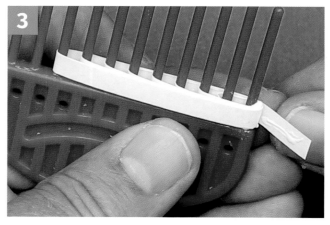

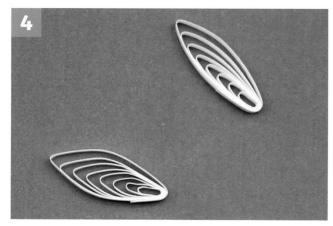

1 Hold the quilling comb in one hand. Take one strip of paper and put the end under the comb and up after a minimum of two teeth. Fold the paper over so it meets the start of the comb and add a dab of glue.

2 Fold the long end of the paper strip over the top of the comb and down after the next tooth. Again add a dab of glue.

3 Fold the strip over, and so on until there's no more paper. Cut any excess paper. Take care that the strips are lying straight – you can check by pressing your fingers against the layers now and again as you wind.

4 Slide the paper off the comb.

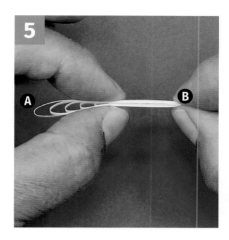

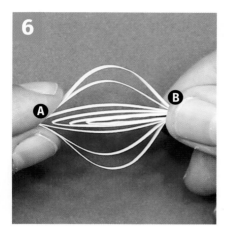

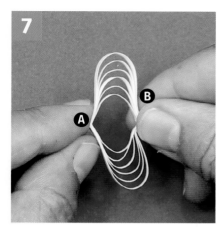

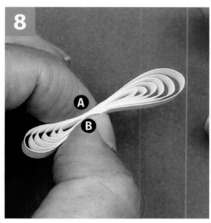

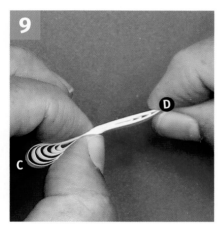

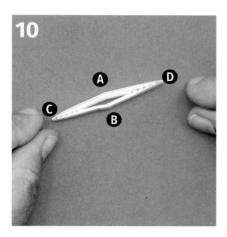

5 Press the strip of paper flat and make ends A and B sharp.

6–7 Now gently press A and B towards each other, taking care that A and B are aligned on top of each other. If you find it difficult, you may have used too much glue!

8 Press A and B together.

9–10 Make ends C and D sharp. You should now have a flattened diamond shape.

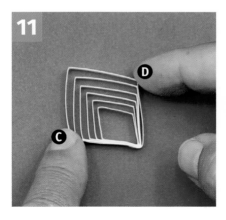

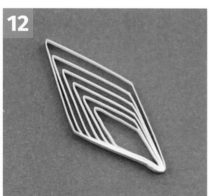

11–12 Press C and D in to create different widths of the diamond shape that is the Galaxy basic.

133

Comb quilling

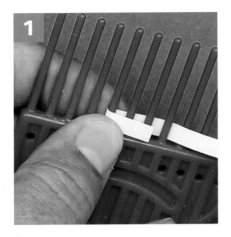

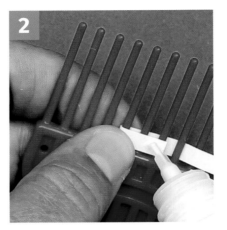

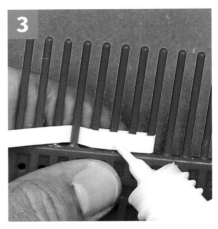

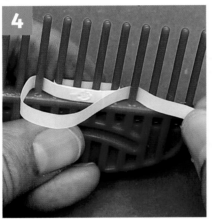

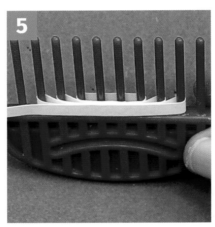

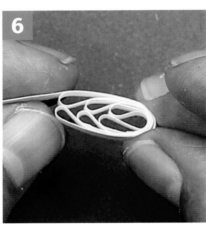

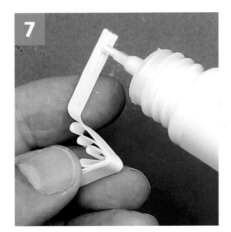

1 Fold the end of a strip of paper over the four teeth in the middle of the quilling comb as shown.

2 Add a dab of glue at the short end and spread with the tip of the glue bottle.

3 Fold the long end over, then down and up again at the next tooth along from where you started. Add a dab of glue.

4 Loop it round, down and up at the next tooth on the opposite side. Take care to ensure the strips are lying neatly upon each other.

5 Continue in this way until you have used all the teeth on the comb and there's a short length of the paper strip left.

6 Fold the strip half and press the loops together gently. It is important to do this quickly, otherwise the glue will dry and they will be too stiff to fold.

7 Add a dab of glue on the tip of the long strip. Fold it over to create a final loop.

Basic shapes

To fill and decorate the basic units that form the stars, different shapes are used.

Tight coil

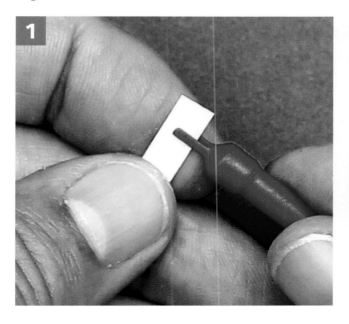

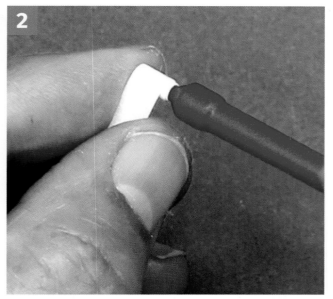

1 Thread the paper strip through the slot of your quilling pen. Leave about ³⁄₁₆in (5mm) sticking out.

2 Now roll it away from yourself. After rolling for three or four rounds, place your thumb and index finger like a pair of pincers at each side of the paper roll. Keep rolling – firm, but not too tight;

it must be easy to take the roll off the quilling pen. It can be glued before or after it's taken off the quilling pen. In this book we use the coils as a decorative button shape. To make larger coils you can glue more strips one after the other to make a longer strip.

Laila

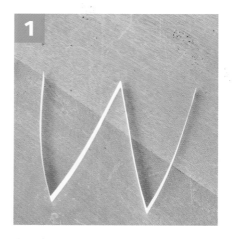

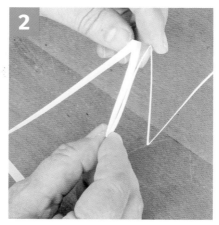

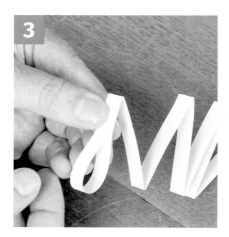

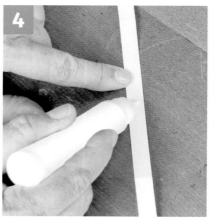

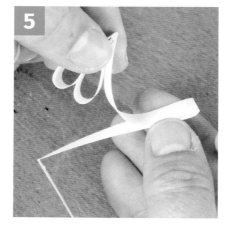

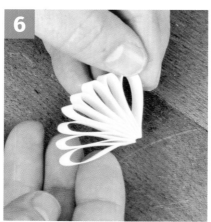

1 Fold a paper strip in half to form a 'V' shape then into quarters to form an 'M' shape. (Note: Never fold with doubled-up paper, as it will not be accurate enough.)

2 Next, fold into eighths in the same way. Make all the folds into mountain folds (i.e. pointing upwards).

3 Loop one end round and add a dab of glue to fix it in position.

4 Unfold the strip. Put a little dab of glue after each fold and at the start.

5–6 Hold the start of the strip between your thumb and index finger and lift each fold up, pressing onto the glue dabs to form consecutive loops.

Antenna

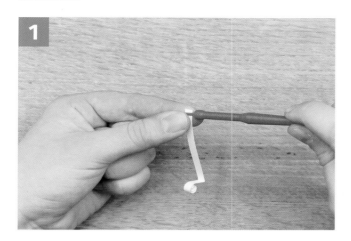

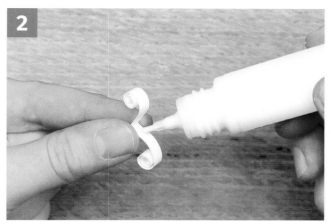

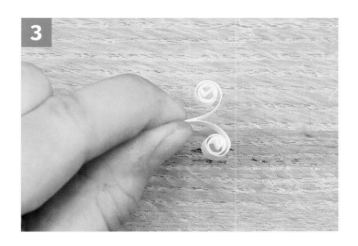

1 Bend the strip in half to form a 'V' shape. Thread one end through the slot of your quilling pen. Leave ³⁄₁₆in–³⁄₈in (5–10mm) sticking out. Now roll away from yourself. After rolling three or four rounds, place your thumb and index finger like a pair of pincers at each side of the paper roll. Keep rolling – firm, but not too

tight; it must be easy to take the roll off the quilling pen. Let the roll spring up. Turn and do the same at the other end of the strip but reverse the direction you wind. Pull the roll to achieve the desired length.

2–3 Glue the middle together to make a stick.

Wings

Make a comb-quillling unit (see page 132), but rather than creating a final loop and gluing the two sides together, simply cut off the excess strip.

Templates

The comb template below enables you to make your own quilling comb. Instructions on how to do this are on pages 124–25. For the quilled designs I recommend using the measuring board templates provided here. They will make the process much easier. The circles help to show where to put the quilled shapes and the coloured lines show where to put the starpoints. You will find full instructions for making the measuring boards are on page 128. If you wish to make stars that are larger than these templates then simply glue them onto a larger piece of paper and draw extended lines.

Quilling comb

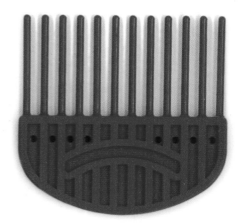

Actual size

1/8 Measuring board template

1 square = ⅜in (10mm)

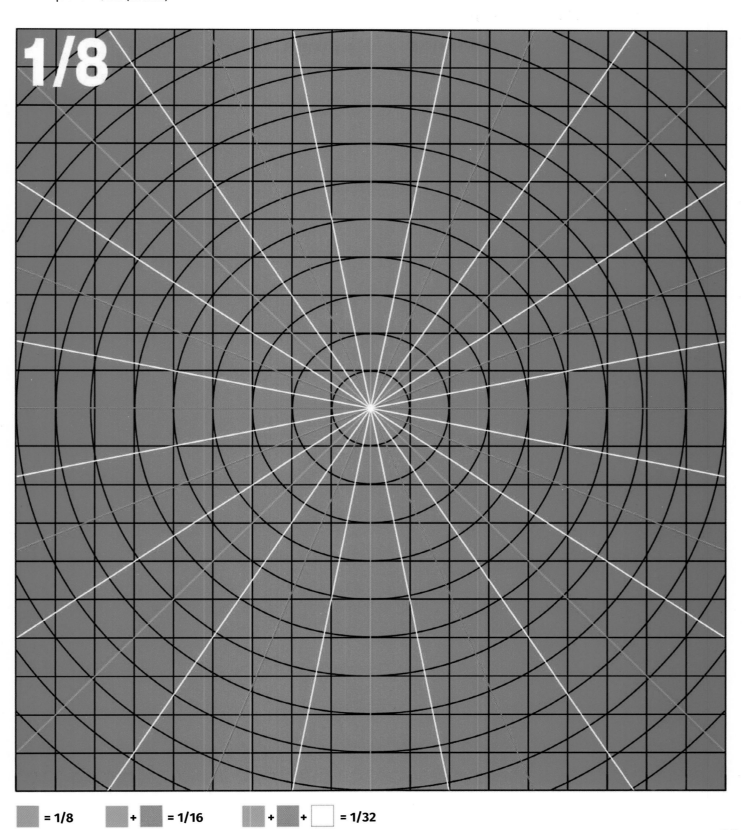

= 1/8   + = 1/16   + + = 1/32

1/6 Measuring Board Template

1 square = ⅜in (10mm)

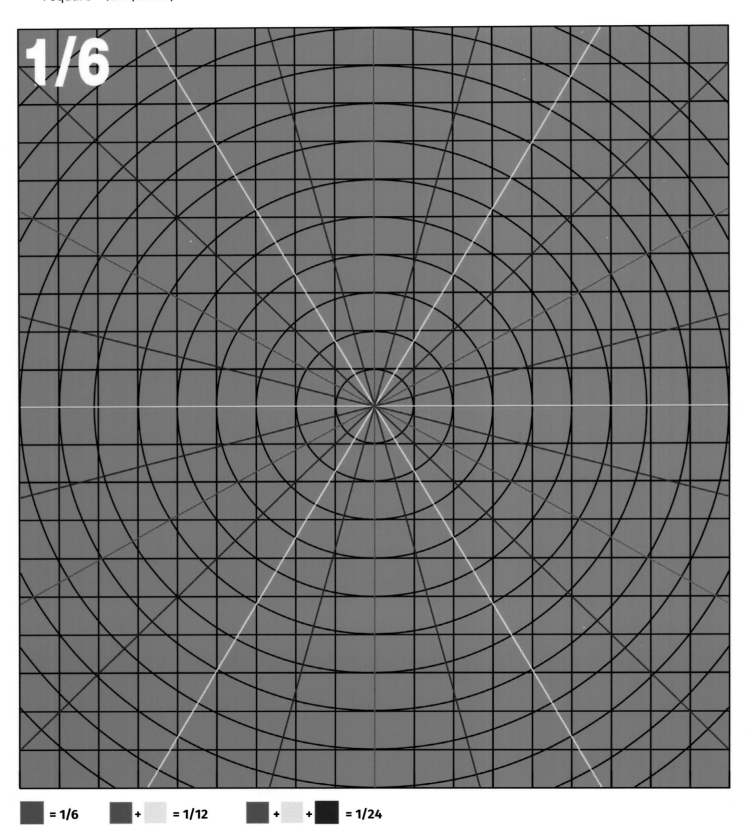

■ = 1/6   ■ + ☐ = 1/12   ■ + ☐ + ■ = 1/24

Suppliers

AUSTRALIA
CraftOnline
Craft Products Australia
13 Advance Road
Kuluin, QLD, 4558
Tel: +69 (1)300 331 311
www.craftonline.com.au

DENMARK
Karen-Marie Klip & Papir
Papirmuseets By A/S
Bomhusvej 3
DK 6300 Gråsten
Tel: +45 74651817
www.karenmarieklip.dk

UK
Hobby Craft
Hobbycraft DC
E-Commerce Door A
Parkway
Centrum 100 Business Park,
Unit 1
Burton Upon Trent
DE14 2WA
Tel: +44 (0)330 026 1400
www.hobbycraft.co.uk

JJ Quilling Design
29 Hollingworth Rd
Orpington BR5 1AQ
Tel: +44 (0)208 295 1822
www.jjquilling.co.uk

USA
Jo-Ann Fabric and Craft Stores
5555 Darrow Rd.
Hudson, OH 44236
Tel: +1 888-739-4120
www.joann.com

Quilled Creations
PO Box 492
Penfield, NY 14526
Tel: +1 585-388-0706
www.quilledcreations.com

Quilling Superstore
6861 Penn Ave
Wernersville, PA 19565
Tel: +1 610-693-4039
www.quillingsuperstore.com

About the author

The Danish paper designer Karen-Marie Fabricius is known for
her stylish paper creations. In 1991 she founded the company Karen-Marie
Klip & Papir. At the heart of her company's concept is a deep fascination with
paper and the endless creative possibilities it offers. Karen-Marie and her
team make the designs, and sell the tools and materials for them from her shop
and webshop in Denmark. The shop, which is designed to look like a small village,
also includes a tiny paper museum and a café.
www.Karenmarieklip.dk

Index

To place an order, or to request a catalogue, contact:
GMC Publications Ltd
Castle Place, 166 High Street, Lewes, East Sussex, BN7 1XU
United Kingdom
Tel: +44 (0)1273 488005
www.gmcbooks.com